FEDERICO PISTONO

ROBOTS WILL STEAL YOUR JOB BUT THAT'S OK

how to survive the economic collapse and be happy

•

With the understanding that:

Waiver – Any of the above conditions can be **waived** if you get permission from the copyright holder.
Public Domain – Where the work or any of its elements is in the **public domain** under applicable law, that status is in no way affected by the license.

Other Rights – In no way are any of the following rights affected by the license:

- Your fair dealing or fair use rights, or other applicable copyright exceptions and limitations;

- The author's moral rights;

- Rights other persons may have either in the work itself or in how the work is used, such as publicity or privacy rights.

Notice – For any reuse or distribution, you must make clear to others the license terms of this work.

Contents

~

"Truly excellent. A very important work. I loved it."

"Thanks for sharing this splendid piece of work. I have never taken drugs, but if I did, I expect that the ride would be like what I experienced in reading your book."

"I really enjoyed it. Accurate stats and good advice. Great notes at the end, very helpful."

"The book's breadth is impressive: its chapters touch on Economics, Sociology, Philosophy, Morality and Artificial Intelligence, and sometimes within the same paragraph. [...] Pistono is trying to construct a future society in which humans will be happy even though they will be less necessary. Instead of an apocalyptic view of the future, Pistono is the rare prophet with a Panglossian view of the future [...] Pistono's book is the refreshing exception: no, we are not doomed. That, per se, is a good reason to read it."

– Piero Scaruffi
autor e historiador cultural
Stanford University

"Understanding the complex relationship between automation and jobs requires empirical analysis and a nuanced inquiry. Federico Pistono's book is a unique and fearless contribution to the ongoing conversation on this topic. He approaches the issues with a perspective that reflects his love of both people and technology [...] Relentlessly constructive, optimistic, and controversial. Read it, then agree or disagree with various points, but join the dialog!"

– Neil Jacobstein
Co-chair AI and Robotics
Singularity University

"WOW – YOU ARE IMPRESSIVE"

– Michael Smolens
Serial Entrepreneur
Founder and Chairman of Dotsub

"Very well written and presented. Quite an accomplishment."

– Kay Koplovitz
Creator of the Sci-Fi Channel
Founder of Springboard Enterprises

Foreword

When at the beginning of 2012 I had been contacted by Federico, asking for the opportunity to exchange ideas, I was glad to consent. From our initial exchange of emails, we quickly proceeded to an online voice and video conversation, and a few days later we agreed to meet in person. He came to visit for a day and stayed a night with me and my family.

Meeting Federico is like letting sunshine into your life. His enthusiasm, curiosity, and passion for his interests and sharing experiences with others make it impossible not to like him. We had a lot of common topics to discuss and it was great to be able to quote books and references to each other and realize that we were studying the same material. We would also mention global movements and organizations to each other and realize that we were both either following their progress or actively participating in them.

This is not only a brief description of the author of this book, and my experiences with him. I think that it is also a glimpse of what more and more people will be able to do, with their time, with their interests. Using technology, and online communications to find people with shared goals. Very rapidly establish shared trust, communicate using flexible tools, and act together to advance joint objectives effectively. An exponential path to human connections!

Robots Will Steal Your Job, But That's OK is a smart, humorous, but thorough, and potentially important approach to a fundamental question of our time. Knowing that Federico is working on it, and that during the summer of 2012 he would have the chance to enrich his views with the experiences that he would have at Singularity University, filled me with excited anticipation. Because, as he describes it in informative and actionable detail, the issues of this book are going to impact billions of people. We are all going to live a future where we will have to redefine our roles, goals, and purpose in life.

Many people are working on various technology solutions to our most pressing problems. And even if we don't have a guarantee, statistically speaking we can rely on one or another of those solutions to be found and then spread quickly. That is why concentrating on people is important: we biological humans can't be easily debugged. Our biases and fallacies are much harder to correct than the

2.0 release of any given gadget. And the process of designing a fruitful future full of wonder must include the largest possible number of people aware of the opportunities we have in front of us. This is why I am so excited that this book is now available and that you have chosen to read it. If you like it, as I hope you will, please make sure to recommend it to your friends who will live, work, and love in the future with you.

– David Orban
CEO of dotSUB
Advisor and Member of the Faculty,
Singularity University
October 2012, New York

Dedication

To all the great people who are dedicating their lives in making the world a better place for everyone.

To the emerging and growing zeitgeist of open science, open education, open culture, creative commons, and the free software movement. You are the heroes of this generation and you give us hope for the future.

Preface

For years, I have been meaning to write a book, but could never bring myself to finish it. Whenever I became interested in a topic, it just opened up an entirely new and unexplored territory, which then lead to another universe of things to discover and understand. The more I searched, the more there was to be found. Every time I believed I had a decent understanding of a topic, something new would arise to challenge my previous assumptions. And so I was back to my studies again.

Maybe it is because I have a questioning nature and too many interests. Sticking to a particular topic for long can be an arduous task for me. In October, 2011, I was traveling throughout Europe, thinking about my future, and preparing a speech for my next conference when I finally decided it was time for change. During a rainy day when I was in Sweden I realised that my goal of a 1,000-page manifesto on how to fix society was unrealistic (and perhaps a bit megalomaniacal). There were too many subjects, all were complex, and I just did not have enough time to tackle them all in one book. I decided that I would pick the most pressing issue and focus on that. Environmental sustainability and climate change came to mind, but there are already many excellent books on these subjects (from people much more qualified than myself). The future of technology and Artificial Intelligence was another, but the same conclusion applied. Then I realised that one of the most pressing issues we are going to face, both as individuals and as societies, is being deeply overlooked. Technology is displacing human labour.

Up until now, very few authors have addressed this issue. I was determined to fill this cultural gap. My audience would not occupy the ivory towers of academia – they would mingle in the vibrant crowds of the street. After all, the people most affected by this will be common workers and explanations of complex subjects in simple, concise, and understandable terms are rare. I promised myself I would create an accessible resource that would be of value to change-makers as well, be they politicians, technophilantropists, or CEOs.

One of the most difficult things for me was to decide what to include and what to leave out. I sincerely hope that I've found the right balance. This is a complex topic and my first book cannot be perfect. Your feedback, both positive and (especially) negative, will help me to improve it in future editions.

I hope this book will make you think about your future, guide you in understanding the world around you a little better, and help you navigate the endless sea of ever-changing wonders. And while you are at it, it might make you smile a bit and become slightly happier.

If I succeed in doing that, then the time and effort I put in writing this book was well spent.

Acknowledgements

When I launched this book project, bearing that in mind I wanted to try something different from the typical routine of book publishing. Call it a social experiment. Instead of going through the usual process of trying to get an agent, to then maybe get an offer from a publishing company, to then get a 10% share of the sales at best (if all goes well), I decided to take a radically different route.

I figured that I write for the people who will read the book, not for the publishers. If people believe in me and in the project, they will show their support. If the don't, so be it. Naturally, it is a bit harder to go solo than it is to rely on someone else. You have to continuously prove your credibility, build a fan base, give interviews, write articles, manage your own promotion, and create a trust relationship with your audience.

I decided to go with the crowdfunding site IndieGoGo and in just a few weeks 78 people decided to support my project, exceeding my initial funding goal by 130%. This gave me the chance to hire a professional designer for the book cover and send a few books to friend as presents.

The very first published version of this book contained some spelling mistakes and was in dire need of additional proofreading. The current revision (January 2014, the one you are reading now) should have all of that fixed, and for that I must thank my friends Immanuel Otto and Adam Waterhouse.

On my site (http://robotswillstealyourjob.com/supporters) there is a list of those forward thinking individuals who supported me during the campaign. Among them, a few stood out as particularly generous, so I would like to especially thank Ben McLeish, Marco Bassetti, Daniele Mancinelli, Mark Henson, Justin Gress, Eric Ezechieli, and Jonathan Jarvis.

Then to all my friends who gave invaluable advice, both in "real life"[1] and in the virtual world, and to my Facebook fans and twitter followers.

Thank you all.

You are awesome.

Introduction

You are about to become obsolete. You think you are special, unique, and that whatever it is that you are doing is impossible to replace. You are wrong. As we speak, millions of algorithms created by computer scientists are frantically running on servers all over the world, with one sole purpose: do whatever humans can do, but better. These algorithms are intelligent computer programs, permeating the substrate of our society. They make financial decisions, they predict the weather, they predict which countries will wage war next. Soon, there will be little left for us to do: machines will take over.

Does that sound like some futuristic fantasy? Perhaps. This argument is proposed by a growing yet still fringe community of thinkers, scientists, and academics, who see the advancement of technology as a disruptive force, which will soon transform our entire socioeconomic system forever. According to them, the displacement of labour by machines and computer intelligence will increase dramatically over the next few decades. Such changes will be so drastic and quick that the market will be unable to create new opportunities for workers who have lost their jobs, making unemployment not just part of a cycle, but structural in nature and chronically irreversible. It will be the end of work as we know it.

Most economists discard such arguments. Many of them don't even address the issue in the first place. And those who do address this issue claim that the market always finds a way. As machines replace old jobs, new jobs are created. Thanks to the ingenuity of the human mind and the need for growth, markets always find a way, especially in the ever-connected and globalised mass market we live in today.

In this book I will try to avoid picking either side based on belief, gut feeling, or hunch. Rather, I will attempt to engage in informed logical reasoning, based on the evidence we have so far.

The book is divided into three parts. First, we will explore the topic of technological unemployment and its impact on work and society? I chose to focus on the US economy, but the same argument applies to most of the industrialised world. In the second part we will look into the nature of work itself and the relationship between work and happiness. The last part is a bold attempt to provide some practical suggestions on how to deal with the issues presented in the first two parts. Doing a thorough examination of each section would require a monumental effort, possibly resulting in thousands of pages, far exceeding the purpose of this book. My intention is not to write a complete academic report, but rather to initiate a discussion about what I think will soon be one of the biggest challenges that we have to face as a society and as individuals. Too often we treat various issues as separate subjects, not realising the interconnected nature of our reality. This mistake has made us weak and vulnerable. Over the last 70 years, we have set the stage of our own demise. We have become increasingly discontent, the quality of our relationships have diminished, and we have lost track of what really matters. Today, as the comedian Louis CK has noted: ?Everything is amazing, and nobody is happy!? It is time to take a step back and think about where we are going.

Let us begin the journey.

Part I

Automation and Unemployment

CHAPTER 1

UNEMPLOYMENT TODAY

We usually get a sense of how good (or how bad) things are by reading the news and by looking at the world around us. We see how we live, we talk to our neighbours, we read newspapers, blogs, tweets, and watch TV. Very few people find the time to check for themselves the long and boring tables from the OECD Factbook, or the US Bureau of Labor Statistics. The business columns in newspapers are often filled with financial jargon, which does not really facilitate a clear understanding of what is happening for those who are not familiar with the intricacies of the economic system. As a result, most people do not have a clue about what is *really* going on. A quick glance at the recent statistics about job growth in the United States and in Europe should make us a bit concerned, to say the least.

In July 2011, the US Government released a report showing that 117,000 new jobs had been created that month, and the New York Times featured a promising headline "US Posts Stronger Solid Growth in July".[2] But, an ugly truth was hidden behind this veil of false hope. A growth of 117,000 jobs was not even enough to make up for population growth (about 130,000 people every month), let alone make a dent on the 12.3 million jobs lost during the 2008-2009 recession. Later in the article, we discover a few more things. The official figure for the unemployment rate was 9.1%, which is already staggeringly high, but it gets even more concerning when considering that an additional 8.4 million people were working part-time because they could not find a full-time job, and 1.1 million had become so discouraged that they had stopped looking for work altogether. If we include these people, the broader measure of unemployment was 16.1% in July 2011. Please take a moment and let that sink in. The United States of America, possibly the wealthiest country in the world, had an unemployment rate at 16.1% as recent as July 2011.

As if that was not enough, it turns out that only 58.1% of the population was working, the lowest level in nearly three decades.[3] Laura D'Andrea Tyson,

Professor at the Haas School of Business at the University of California, Berkeley, calculated that even if we could somehow create 208,000 new jobs per month, every month, for the foreseeable future, it would still take until 2023 to fill that gap.[4] In January 2012, thanks to massive efforts from both the private sector and the government, the unemployment rate fell to 8.3%.[5] A very mild consolation, considering that people employed part-time for economic reasons, marginally attached to the labor force, discouraged workers, and the long-term unemployed changed very little over the year. To make things even worse, the labour force participation rate is 63.7%, its all time lowest since 1983, when women had not entered the work force in large numbers, and it is dropping consistently every year.[6]

MIT Economists Erik Brynjolfsson and Andrew McAfee make a lucid analysis of this problem in their book *Race Against The Machine: How the Digital Revolution is Accelerating Innovation, Driving Productivity, and Irreversibly Transforming Employment and the Economy*[7], which deals with the current unemployment crisis and tries to offer some solutions, particularly by reforming education, the system of economic incentives, and by promoting entrepreneurship. While I concur with their analysis, I think their solutions are limited to the way things have worked until now. They appear to be assuming that the system of economic incentives, what drives people, and human nature itself are almost immutable. According to Voltaire, "Work spares us from three evils: boredom, vice, and need", and having a job has undoubtedly been the driving force to combat them up until now. However, I challenge the assumption that this is the only way we can do that, and we shall explore why in the coming chapters.

Other authors have addressed the same issue. Jeremy Rifkin was one of the first to seriously consider this problem. In 1995 he published *The End of Work: The Decline of the Global Labor Force and the Dawn of the Post-Market Era*[8], where he predicted that worldwide unemployment would increase as information technology eliminates tens of millions of jobs in the manufacturing, agricultural, and service sectors. He traced the devastating impact of automation on blue-collar, retail and wholesale employees: "While a small elite of corporate managers and knowledge workers reap the benefits of the high-tech world economy, the American middle class continues to shrink and the workplace becomes ever more stressful"[9]. While he may have gotten some of the details wrong, the general outline is so spot-on that it seems almost prophetic. Over the past twenty years we have witnessed the gradual disappearance of the American middle class, with rising costs and lower income[10,11], while the wealthiest Americans have accumulated more wealth than ever before in history.

To get an idea of the disproportionate amount of wealth generated by the system, how unevenly distributed it is, and exactly how it had steadily become worse since 1979, let us look at the following graphs[12].

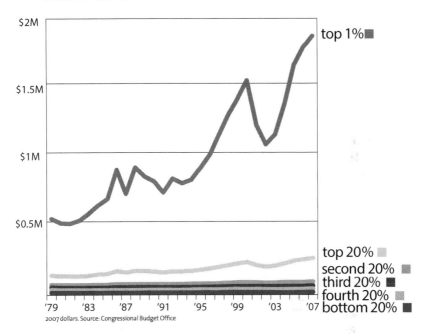

Figure 1.1: Average Household Income

As you can see from Figure 1.1, average household income had remained pretty much the same for well over 80% of the population, while the top 1% experienced a tremendous increase, particularly starting in 1994. Even more revealing is the change in share of income, calculated *after* taxes (Figure 1.2).

The lower 80% have actually seen a substantial decrease of income, while the very top has hardly been affected. what is even more worrying is the distortion in the public perception of this phenomenon, even after the worldwide Occupy Movement broke out.

A 2011 paper by Harvard Professor Michael Norton and Duke University Professor Dan Ariely, called *Building a Better America – One Wealth Quintile at a Time* shows just how skewed our perception is.[13]

History proved Rifkin right. The middle class is disappearing, the richest are getting richer, and we have no idea how bad the situation truly is. The question is, was Rifkin right about work and automation, too?

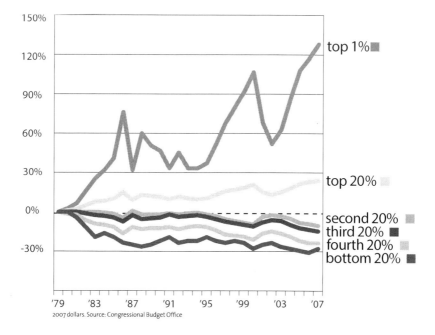

Figure 1.2: Change in share of income 1979-2007, calculated after taxes.

Martin Ford followed up on this, utilising his entrepreneurial and software engineering perspective. His 2009 book *The Lights in the Tunnel: Automation, Accelerating Technology and the Economy of the Future* aims to show how automation will inevitably lead to structural unemployment, and millions of people, both skilled and unskilled workers, will soon find themselves out of the workforce, with little to no chance of getting back in. Ford has since written many articles on major news websites, thereby bringing the issue of technological unemployment back into the public eye. He was also a source of inspiration to me when I decided to write this book. However, as with Brynjolfsson's book, I do not think his solutions are feasible; nor, in most cases, desirable.

All of these authors have identified a real problem and they've tried to propose viable solutions to that problem using their knowledge, skills, analysis, and background. But as I read their books, I felt there was something missing. Something was not accounted for. I felt they were trying to find solutions in a context where solutions were nowhere to be found.

Before I continue, let us be clear on something. All of the authors I just

Out of Balance

A Harvard business prof and a behavioral
economist recently asked more than
5,000 Americans how they thought
wealth is distributed in the United States.
Most thought that it's more balanced
than it actually is. Asked to choose their
ideal distribution of wealth, 92% picked
one that was even more equitable.

top 20%
second 20%
third 20%
fourth 20%
bottom 20%

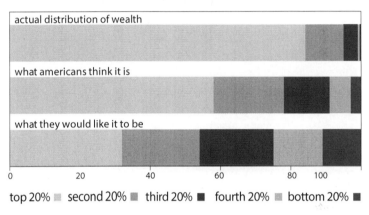

Source: Michael I. Norton, Harvard Business School; Dan Ariely, Duke University

Figure 1.3: *Building a Better America – One Wealth Quintile at a Time*, Michael I. Norton,
Dan Ariely. Journal Perspectives on Psychological Science.

mentioned are highly qualified and intelligent professionals, with much more
academic and working experience than myself. That is not in question. But they
were not born into a culture where things changed dramatically in just a few
years. They had to adapt to the idea of rapid change, they were not born in a
generation that created this massive accelerating change. I was lucky enough
to be part of that generation. I have seen the free and Open Source movement
rise and become one of the greatest forces on the planet. The dreams I had
when I was a child of small groups of dedicated and intelligent people changing
the world, have come true. It has been exhilarating to witness these events,
which are becoming even more ubiquitous, as their rampant increase terrifies
the establishment and excites the revolutionaries.

Perhaps I am wrong and all of this comes from the arrogant, blissful ignorance of youth. But perhaps there is something true that transcends me as an individual and speaks through me. It is the collective intelligence of all the people I have spoken with, all the books I have read, the experiences I've had in the ever-connected cybernetic organism known as the Internet. I do not pretend to be the voice of my generation, or that of the entire Web for that matter. But it is undeniable that these intelligences have shaped me, influenced me, and directed me over the years. And now I am simply remixing what I received. This is social evolution: copy, transform, and combine.[14]

However, there is also another possibility. It is entirely conceivable that we are all wrong, myself and those authors. Mainstream economists and analysts could be right. It may be that we do not understand some basic economic concepts, and that our analyses are nothing more than a fallacy, which could be easily solved by getting our economics right and by studying the past a little bit more. After all, we have seen unemployment fluctuate up and down for hundreds of years, only to go back to familiar levels, without any substantial change in the structure of the economy. As new technologies come along, we cyclically move from one sector to another, creating new jobs, and everything works just fine. Economists have a name for this phenomenon, which takes us back a long time. So, before I go any further, let me tell you a story.

CHAPTER 2

THE LUDDITE FALLACY

We are in England, at the end of the 18th century. A boy named Ned Ludd is a weaver from the village of Anstey, just outside Leicester. He does not know it yet, but he is about to make history.

It is a hard and laborious day in 1779, Ludd is apprenticed to learn framework knitting. But he is averse to confinement or work, and refuses to exert himself. His master is displeased and complains to a magistrate, who orders a whipping. In response, Ludd grabs a hammer and demolishes the hated frame. This act will be told by generations to come, and Ludd became history. Or so the story goes.

As with every myth, there are many variations of the story. Some accounts say that Ludd was told by his father, a framework-knitter, to 'square his needles'. Ludd took a hammer and 'beat them into a heap'. Other stories can also be found, and nobody really knows which one is true, if any[15].

Whether or not any of it really happened is irrelevant. What matters is that news of the incident, like every good folk story, was spread and distorted. Whenever frames were sabotaged, people would jokingly say, "Ned Ludd did it". His actions inspired the folkloric character of Captain Ludd, also known as King Ludd or General Ludd, who became the alleged leader and founder of a movement called, not surprisingly, 'The Luddites'.

The Luddites can be traced back to Nottingham, England, around 1811. It was composed mostly of hosiery and lace workers, English textile artisans who protested against the changes produced by the Industrial Revolution – often by destroying mechanised looms. They smashed knitting machines that embodied new labour-saving technology as a protest against unemployment. Simply put, machines were stealing their jobs, and they did not like where that was going.

People began to speculate whether this was the beginning of an irreversible process, or if things would go back to normal. At the time automation was represented by no more than a steam-engine machine, something that could have hardly been seen as a realistic replacement for human labour in general. However, some suggested that the problem of machine automation could exacerbate in a few years, putting the very companies that produced goods at risk. Industrialist Henry Ford understood this quite profoundly. In fact, he paid his workers twice the going rate, so that they could afford to buy the cars that they themselves were producing.[16]

This makes sense. You need people to have enough money to buy the products you create, otherwise the cycle of production-consumption is interrupted. If automation replaces humans faster than they can find new occupations, you have a problem. As a result, people may get upset, and start to jeopardise machines, in order to ensure their workers not lose their job. To this day, we still call these people "Luddites".

Neoclassical economists have dismissed such proposition as nonsense. They claim that this argument is a fallacy. Economist Alex Tabarrok famously said in 2003:

> If the Luddite fallacy were true we would all be out of work because productivity has been increasing for two centuries.[17]

And if you look around you, it would seem that the Luddite argument is indeed a fallacy. By studying the historical record, one should be pretty optimistic about the future of the economy. Automation and mechanisation have consistently been introduced, and that led to an increase in productivity. More work could be made, with less labour. More products were coming out of our factories. More wealth was generated. But the total requirement for labour did not decrease. As the economy grew, so did our standard of living. And our perception of what is necessary for a comfortable life changes accordingly. A hundred years ago, even the richest man in the world could not even dream of owning a small electronic device that could connect him with whomever he liked, anywhere in the world. Today, not owning a cell phone is inconceivable to most people. Even in the poorest countries, people have access to cell phones. A boy in a village in rural Africa with a cell phone (you would be surprised of how many of them do) has access to more information than the president of the United States did 20 years ago. Some have gone so far as to argue that the poorest of today are richer than the richest kings of the past. I would not agree with that, because many times it is cheaper to obtain these technological marvels than it is to find food. You get the idea.

Over the past two centuries we have continued to rely on machines to increase our productivity, but we have not been displaced by them. On the contrary, we created new jobs, new sectors, and new opportunities. Machines allowed us to become more creative, more productive. As we moved from the agricultural to the manufacturing sector, and then to the services, we began to expand our domination of the planet.

So, if the idea that automation creates unemployment is a fallacy, then there is nothing to worry about. The staggering rate of unemployment that we are experiencing today in 2012 (8.2% in the US, 24.1% in Spain, 21.7% in Greece, 14.5% in Ireland[18]) is just one of the many cycles of the economy. Or it may be due to bad policies. Or bad politicians. Or the financial bubble of subprime mortgages that burst a couple of years ago. Maybe it is a combination of all of them. If that is the case, then we just need to elect better politicians, demand better reforms, and reduce the influence of the financial sector on the economy. In other words, it could be just a matter of time before things go back to normal. Get back on your feet, work hard, and everything will be fixed. I would like to believe that. I really would. But the reality may be very different.

While these resolutions are certainly good ideas, and they are necessary for creating a better society in which to live, they might not be sufficient. In fact, it might be that no matter how hard we try, how good the new wave of politicians are, how resourceful our businesses are, or how ingenious we can be, we will never escape from this crisis. We do not know if that is the case. But it is a possibility, one that we should carefully consider and explore.

Kurt Vonnegut has claimed to have said so much at a private girls school, when he gave a commencement address:[19]

> *Things are going to get unimaginably worse, and they are never, ever, going to get better again.*

I know it is not exactly what you wanted to hear. The rising unemployment levels of the past years could be just the tip of a huge iceberg, and we all could be riding a 21st century economic Titanic. I would like to believe that this is merely unjustified pessimism. But beliefs are heavily influenced by emotions, and the truth does not care what we believe. It just is.

So, how should we approach this conundrum? Will you be the eternal optimist, having faith in the power of the market to adjust itself every time there is a new challenge? Or will you be the incorrigible pessimist, who believes we are doomed, and there is no hope left? Which side will you take?

You see, I do not think it is a matter of picking sides. Or beliefs. Or gut feeling. I would like to take an objective position, as much as possible. I believe in good data, and good logic to interpret that data. I think we should cast aside our ideologies, our personal hunches, and we should use our reason to try and predict the future from an informed perspective. If we want to do that, we are going to have to explore a few things first. These are not difficult ideas. In fact, once explained properly, they are quite simple. But they are also remarkably useful and amazing tools that help us understand the world around us better. Believe it or not, these tools are so basic that they could be easily taught in elementary schools, yet I met many college graduates who failed to apply them at the most fundamental level. Obviously, it is not because these people are not smart enough to understand them, but because they have never been taught to think about the future using these tools.

I will try to explain these ideas to the best of my ability. If I succeed, you will be able to grasp these concepts quite easily, and with them you will see the world from a whole different perspective. You will have all the necessary tools to approach this challenging task, and make up your own mind about which side of the debate you should take. From there, we will take off, think about the future, and see how to live better accordingly.

Let us get started.

CHAPTER 3

EXPONENTIAL GROWTH

One of the most important, yet misunderstood concepts in our lives, is the nature of the exponential function. You may have heard of this term before. Maybe it was mentioned in some newspaper article in the technology section, briefly cited and hardly explained at all. Or perhaps under the name "compound interest" when you took out a loan from your bank. Of course, they usually tend to gloss over its real significance, and rarely does someone explain what it really means. Yet, it pervades every facet of our lives, the economy, and the decisions we will have to make in the future. Understanding the power of the exponential function is key in proceeding further with the analysis presented in this book.

Albert Bartlett, Professor emeritus of Physics at University of Colorado-Boulder, during a very famous lecture he gave, stated that "the greatest shortcoming of the human race is our inability to understand the exponential function."[20] This is no light statement. Professor Bartlett has lectured over 1,600 times since 1969 on Arithmetic, Population, and Energy, trying to warn as many people as possible about the dangers in failing to understand this most important concept.

Before the end of this chapter, I want you to have a clear understanding of the exponential function. It does not matter whether you have a degree in philosophy, in economics, if you are a college dropout, if you are uneducated, unemployed, if you are a Professor at university, or the CEO of a multinational corporation; chances are you do not fully understand what exponential growth really means. Yet, it is imperative that you do.

I've given many lectures during my life, to all kinds of audiences. Even among the most educated ones, people fell short when confronted with very simple examples of exponential growth. -However, when properly explained, everyone was able to understand it. This gives me hope, because it is crucial that everybody realises what it means, and what the consequences are of applying steady exponential growth in the years to come.

Enough with my ramblings, are you ready? Good. Let us dig in and see what it is all about.

The exponential function is used to describe the size of anything growing steadily over time. For example, suppose you have to buy a house, and the bank gives you a loan at 7% interest. What it means is that every year the amount of money you have to give back grows by 7%. The first year the quantity grows by a tiny amount (turning the debt to a total of 107% of the principle), but on the second year it grows relative to the last amount, not to the original principle. So, 7% of 107%. The following year it grows even more, and so it goes. Can you guess what the amount will be in 20 years? Not too easy, unless you have taken statistics in college. It is not my intention to explore the mathematics of the exponential function (although it is really interesting and I suggest that some of you do). I want you to understand it in very clear and effective terms, so I will give you a simple formula that you can use any time, anywhere, and all you need is first-grade math. If you want to know how long will it take to double any quantity that grows at a fixed rate, take the number 70 and divide it by the rate of growth[21]. This is called the doubling time:

$$\text{Doubling time} = \frac{70}{\text{rate of constant growth}}$$

Let us go back to our example. Growth was 7% per year. It did not sound too impressive before, did it? Now, take 70, divide it by 7, it gives us 10. That means that circa every 10 years the amount of money we owe to the bank will double.

That looked easy enough, did not it? Well, that is because it is. It is a simple calculation, one that a 10-year old can do without breaking a sweat, and yet most politicians, policy-makers, urban planners, and economists worldwide fail to understand it. To be fair, any economist must have taken a statistics course at university, and the rule of 70 (or one of its variations[22]) is widely known among academics, so they know about it. But while the calculation may be easy to do, the implications of doubling over time are far less obvious and very misunderstood.

So far we have seen what it takes to double the principle. Now, let us explore the effect of this doubling over time. Suppose we borrowed $100,000 from the bank at 7% interest. As we have seen before, in just 10 years we will owe $200,000, or double the principle. But how about in 20 years? It will not be $300,000, but instead $400,000, which is two times the previous amount of $200,000 (which was itself twice the principle). How about in 30 years? You got it, $800,000! Ten more years, it is already $1.6 million. A few more years and you will owe more than you could ever make in your entire life. Luckily, most loans do not exceed the 30-year mark. But what would happen for other things, things that are not mortgage loans, and that may grow far more than 30 years? Buckle your seatbelt because we are just getting started.

3.1 EXPLOSIVE POWER

The idea of exponential growth is not new at all. In fact, it goes back thousands of years. Legend has it that when the creator of the game of chess (some say it was an ancient Indian mathematician[23]) showed his invention to the ruler of the country, the king was so pleased that he gave the inventor the right to name his prize for the invention. The man, who was very wise, asked the king this: that for the first square of the chess board, he would receive one grain of wheat, on the following day two for the second square, on the day after that four on the third one, and so forth, doubling the amount each time. The king, who had no idea of the power of the exponential function, quickly accepted the inventor's offer, even getting offended by his perceived notion that the inventor was asking for such a low prize, and ordered the treasurer to count and hand over the wheat to the inventor over the coming days. A few days pass by and the inventor receives only a handful of grain, and the king is somewhat baffled. After a week, the inventor started bringing home big bags of wheat. A few days after that... you see where this is going, right? We start with 1, the next day we double, so we have 2 grains. The next day is 4 grains. Then 8, 16, 32, 64, 128, 256, 512... in just 10 days, we went from 1 to 1,024 grains. 10 doublings give you a 1,000-fold increase from the original amount. Here is where things start to take off. 10 more doublings and you have 1 million grains. 10 more: 1 billion grains. Then 1 trillion... we can stop right there. We have already passed the limits of our brain. Figure 3.1 is a graphical representation to describe the process[24]:

On the entire chessboard there would be

$$2^{64} - 1 = 18,446,744,073,709,551,615$$

grains of wheat weighing 461,168,602,000 metric tonnes. That must be a lot of wheat. But just how much wheat are we talking about? More then the king could afford, I can tell you that. In fact, it would be a heap of wheat larger than Mount Everest, earth's highest mountain, with a peak at 8,848 metres (29,029 ft) above sea level. This is around 1,000 times the global production of wheat in 2010 (464,000,000 metric tonnes). That is a lot of wheat. It might very well be more than the entire production of wheat in the history of humanity, combined.

As impressive and incredible as it may sound, we have to remember that this is not just an intriguing fairy tale that we like to tell. It is not merely an intellectual curiosity. It is a story that helps us understand the world around us, and make predictions about how we should go about building our future.

Over the past three years I have given a number of talks, and often I like to play a little game with the audience, to test their comprehension of an exponential increase. Most people do not get it right away, even among the most educated of audiences, so do not feel bad if it does not come to you on the spot.

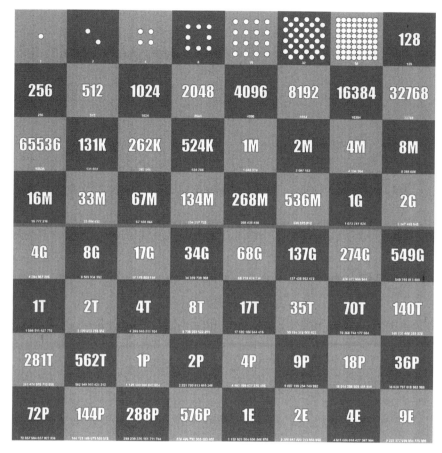

Figure 3.1: Top left, it begins with 1 grain. It goes on to the right with 2, 4, 8, 16... then numbers grow too big, we start to use the binary notation: K=kilo (1 thousand), M = Mega (1 million), G = Giga (1 billion), T = Tera (1 trillion), P = Peta (1 quadrillion), E = Exa (1 quintillion).

Imagine an empty glass of water (technically a glass is made of glass and is full of air, but please bear with the limitations of our language). Place some bacteria inside, and let them replicate, by giving them food. The replication process is such that the number of bacteria doubles every minute. After 60 minutes, the glass is full, and since there is no more space left for food, the bacteria die. The question is: what percentage of the glass did the bacteria fill after 55 minutes?

How much would you say? Take a pencil and use this empty page to scribble, sketch, and do some calculations. The answer is on the next page, but I strongly encourage you to have fun and try it out for yourself first.

Scribble, sketch, and have fun!

Figure 3.2: On the left, at minute zero, there are no bacteria in the glass. On the right, after a certain amount of doublings, the bacteria filled the whole thing. But what happens at minute 55 (in the centre)?

I hope you did try to solve it yourself, because learning is so much more fulfilling when it is interactive. If you did not, too bad for you. ☹

In truth, the bacteria have only filled 3.125% of the glass. But how can this be? Well it is simple. If they double every minute, and they fill the entire glass in 60 minutes, then they will have filled half the glass the minute before 60 (or 50% after 59 minutes), half of that the minute before 59 (or 25% after 58 minutes), and so on. Table 3.1 summary of the last 10 minutes, starting from the end.

It all makes sense now, right? Suddenly it becomes clear, even obvious. Who could not get this? It is so simple, right? Apparently, it is not. The most common replies I get are between 50% and 90%. Even college graduates typically get it wrong. And let?s not talk about politicians.

We will come back to this in the Appendix, with some real-world examples. For now, I think it is safe to say that we all understand what steady growth means. Let's now see how this applies to our main focus in the next chapter: information technology.

Time Elapsed	Amount Filled
60 minutes	100.000%
59 minutes	50.000%
58 minutes	25.000%
57 minutes	12.500%
56 minutes	6.250%
55 minutes	3.125%
54 minutes	1.563%
53 minutes	0.781%
52 minutes	0.391%
51 minutes	0.195%

Table 3.1: Exponential growth of bacteria in a bottle over the last 10 minutes.

CHAPTER 4

INFORMATION TECHNOLOGY

Now that we have a solid understanding of the exponential function, we can begin to look at things from a more informed perspective. You may have heard of Moore's Law, which states that the number of transistors that can be placed on an integrated circuit doubles approximately every two years. This effectively means that computer power doubles every 24 months or so. When Gordon E. Moore, co-founder of Intel Corporation, the world's largest semiconductor chip manufacturer, described this trend in his famous 1965 paper,[25] people were very sceptical. He noticed that the number of components in integrated circuits had doubled every year from the invention of the integrated circuit in 1958 until 1965, and predicted that the trend would continue ?"for at least ten years." Many did not believe him. They said it was an inaccurate prediction. We could not expect it to grow any further, due to various technical problems. Those sceptics were wrong. In fact, it has been doubling steadily for more than 50 years, without any sign of stopping. But Moore's Law is not the whole story. The exponential expansion of technology has been growing remarkably smoothly for a much longer time, and integrated circuits are just a tiny fraction of the whole spectrum of change that pervades technological advancement.

Ray Kurzweil notes[26] that Moore's Law of Integrated Circuits was not the first, but rather the fifth paradigm to provide accelerating price-performance. Computing devices have been consistently multiplying in power (per unit of time), from the mechanical calculating devices used in the 1890 US Census, to Turing's relay-based Bombe machine that cracked the Nazi enigma code, to the CBS vacuum tube computer that predicted the election of Eisenhower, to the transistor-based machines used in the first space launches, to the integrated-circuit-based personal computer which Kurzweil used to dictate the very essay that described this phenomenon, in 2001.

To get an idea of what exponential growth means, look at the following graph, which represents the difference between a linear trend and an exponential one.

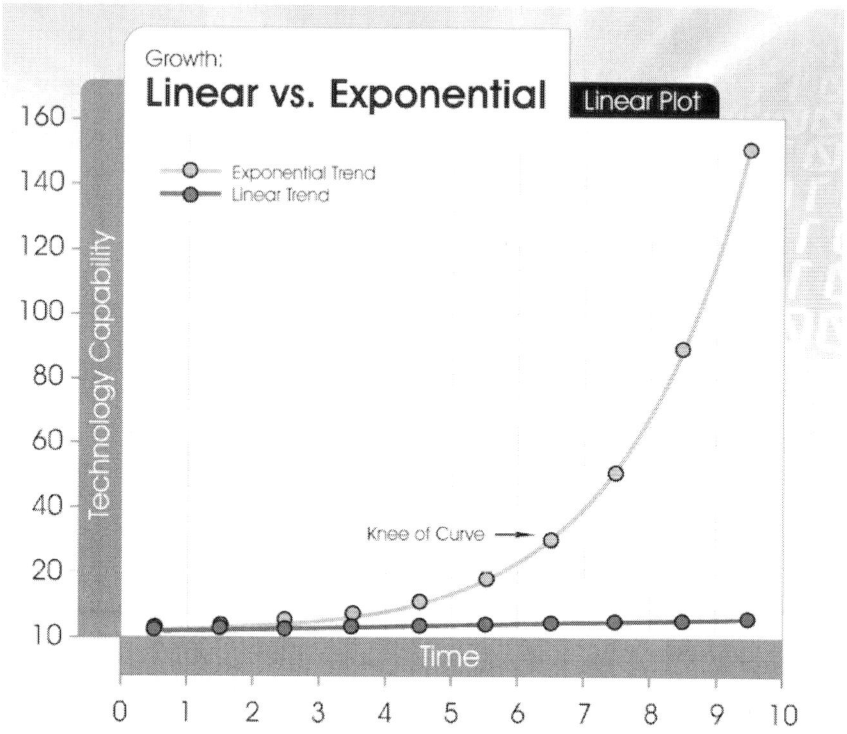

Figure 4.1: The difference between a Linear and an Exponential curve. Courtesy of Ray Kurzweil.

As you can see, the exponential trend starts to really take off where the 'Knee of the Curve' begins. Before that, things do not seem to change significantly. It is just like the story of the chess board and the king. In the first few days nothing notable happens, but as soon as the curve kicks in, something dramatic happens and things go out of control.

If we were to plot the same graph on a logarithmic scale, the line representing the exponential trend – which soon got out of control in the first graph – would look much more manageable. On the y-axis (vertical), representing quantity, instead of moving 20–40–60, we would move 10–100–1,000. So, a curve that would normally go right off the ceiling on a linear graph will look like a straight line on a logarithmic plot. You will understand why we utilise logarithms when talking about exponentials – without them there simply is not enough space to show the curve.

What is even more remarkable is that, when Kurzweil plotted the world's fastest calculator's on a graph since 1900, he noticed something quite surprising. Remember that a straight line on a logarithmic graph means exponential growth? If you thought exponential growth was fast, you haven?t seen anything yet. Take a look at this graph.

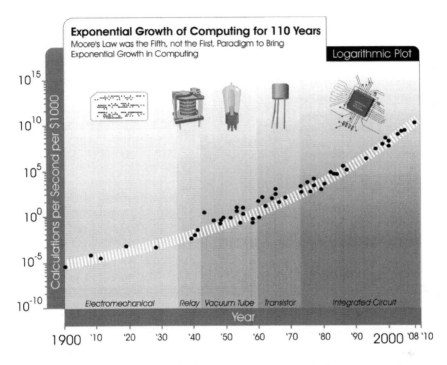

Figure 4.2: The Exponential Growth of computing power over the last 110 years. Courtesy of Ray Kurzweil.

This plot is logarithmic. You can see the y-axis having the number 10 growing at five orders of magnitude after each step (that is a 100,000 fold increase every time!), but the curve is not a straight line. Instead, what you see is an upward trend. What this means is that there is another exponential curve. In other words, there is exponential growth in the rate of exponential growth. Considering what we have just learned about exponential growth, I would say that that is pretty remarkable. Computer speed (per unit cost) doubled every three years between 1910 and 1950, then doubled every two years between 1950 and 1966, and is now doubling every year. Computer power is not simply increasing. It is increasing faster and faster, every year.

According to the available evidence, we can infer that this trend will continue for the foreseeable future, or at least another 30 years. Eventually, it will hit physical limits imposed by the laws of nature, and its increase will have to slow down. Some suggest that we may be able to circumvent that problem, once the singularity is reached.

Technological Singularity refers to the time when the speed of technological change is so fast that we are unable to predict what will happen. At that moment, computer intelligence will exceed that of human, and we will not even be able to understand what changes are happening. The term was first coined by science fiction writer Vernon Vinge and subsequently popularised by many authors, predominantly Ray Kurzweil with his books *The Age of Spiritual Machines* and *The Singularity is Near*. This idea, however, is highly speculative, and it is far beyond the purpose of this book to examine its feasibility. Suffice to say that in order for machines to replace most human jobs, the singularity is not a necessary requirement, as we will see in the next chapters. Whether you buy into the singularity argument or not doesn?t matter. The data is clear, facts are facts, and we only have to look a few years into the future to reach conclusions that are alarming enough.

The **Turing Test** is a thought experiment proposed in 1950 by the brilliant English mathematician and father of computers, Alan Turing. Imagine you enter a room where a computer sits on top of a desk. You notice there is a chat window and two conversations are open. As you begin to type messages down, you are told you are in fact talking to one person and one machine. You can take as much time as you want to find out which is which. If you are not able to tell the difference between them, the machine is said to have passed the test.

There are many variations of the same experiment, you could have more interlocutors, and they could all be machines, or they could all be humans, and you might be tricked into thinking otherwise. Whatever the flavour, the main idea is clear: you conduct conversations through natural language to determine if you are communicating with a human or a computer. A machine able to pass the Turing test is said to have achieved human-level intelligence, or at least perceived intelligence (whether we consider that to be true intelligence or not is irrelevant for the purpose of the argument). Some people call this Strong Artificial Intelligence (Strong AI), and many see Strong AI as an unachievable myth, because the brain is mysterious, and so much more than the sum of its individual components. They claim that the brain operates using unknown, possibly unintelligible quantum mechanical processes, and any effort to reach or even surpass it using mechanical machines is pure fantasy. Others claim that the brain is just a biological machine, not much different from any other machine, and that it is merely a matter of time before we can surpass it using our artificial creations. This is certainly a fascinating topic, one that would require a thorough examination. Perhaps I will explore it in another book. For now, let us concentrate on the present, on what we know for sure, and on the upcoming future. As we will see, there is no need for machines to achieve Strong AI in order to change the nature of the economy, employment, and our lives, forever.

We will start by looking at what intelligence is, how it can be useful, and if machines have become intelligent, perhaps even more so than us.

CHAPTER 5

INTELLIGENCE

There is a great deal of confusion regarding the meaning of the word "intelligence??, mainly because nobody really knows what it is. There are attempts to define this word, but they fall short when confronted by logic and informed questions. The Oxford English dictionary defines it as follows:

Intelligence [ɪnˈtɛlɪdʒəns]: *The ability to acquire and apply knowledge and skills.*

Given this very broad definition, one can easily include animals, particularly great apes, into the category of "intelligent" beings. We can also include computer programs. Think of Google. It acquires knowledge (crawls web pages) and applies skills (returns search results based on the knowledge acquired). A hint of what it means to be intelligent could emerge from the very etymology of the word, as it comes from Latin *intellegentia*, or "the act of choosing between" Hence, we could update the definition to "the ability to acquire knowledge, apply skills, and make informed choices"

Most people, when using common sense, would not regard machines to be "intelligent" in any way. Sure, they can make choices based on deterministic algorithms or probabilistic events, but they do not *understand* anything. Machines do not understand what they are doing or *why* they are doing it. It sounds preposterous to use the very word "understand" when dealing with machines. It simply does not apply to them. Whatever they are doing, it is *their* thing, and we are different from them.

This is the argument that is most prevalent among the general public, as well as within academic circles. There is a famous example called *The Chinese Room*[27] that illustrates this concept, but I think it is quite boring. I would like to propose a slightly different one, a personal story.

A few years ago, I was walking through the corridors of my university when I encountered a friend of mine. He seemed quite euphoric, so I asked him what the fuss was all about. He was laughing like crazy and did not reply, which made me even more curious. After catching his breath he said that the scores of the last test were out. See, a few days before he completely forgot we had this test and he took it without being prepared. He used to sleep in class too, so there was no chance of him getting some answers right using common sense.

"Well?" I asked him.

"I had no freaking idea what was going on there. Then I noticed it was a multiple-choice test. I just put AC/DC over and over, top to bottom."

I gave him a *picardian facepalm*.[28] Then he cracked up again. "Dude, I got 87%! Second best in the class!".

What can we learn from this anecdote? The dubious hypothesis of divine intervention by the God of heavy metal aside, it is clear he did not understand anything that was on that test. But to the eyes of the Professor, he was smart. In fact, he was the second smartest person in the whole class, at least as far as that subject was concerned. But just because one gets the answers right, it does not mean that they understood anything. It may be that they got lucky. Or maybe they knew how to mechanistically apply a set of rules to get the results. However if you changed the questions just slightly, they would fail miserably. Some people call this semantics (from Greek *sēmantiká*, neuter plural of *sēmantikós*), which is the study of meaning. But what exactly gives meaning? Can we quantify meaning objectively? I do not think we can. Things, situations, and phrases are all inert. They have no purpose, no intrinsic significance. It is us that gives them meaning. If you do not believe me, try this experiment. Take a €20 bill (or your equivalent) out of your wallet. It is just a piece of paper. A thin layer of cellulose with some ink imprinted on it. By itself, it has no value, no meaning, nor purpose. Now throw it out on the street. I can tell you, it is not going to sit there for long. That is because we give it meaning. We give it value it through a collective agreement. But the paper bill does not really care if it stays there, or if it is picked up.

Now, let us apply this to computers. They can certainly act intelligent. They can get the correct results, in some cases with much better performances than many humans, even with high-level skills such as language manipulation, puns, and musical compositions (more on this later in this chapter). But how can we know if they really mean what they say, or if they understand any of it? I think the answer is that we do not know. And it could be that we cannot know, because the question does not even apply to them.

Maybe intelligence is not an absolute property that exists independent from its environment, and it is us that ultimately sees intelligence in others. Or, as Rodney Brooks put it:[29]

"Intelligence is in the eye of the observer"

This is certainly a fascinating topic to dig into, and several excellent books have been written about it[30]; but it has little relevance when talking about how machine "intelligence" has profoundly changed our culture, and how it will dramatically change our economy and our way of living. From a purely practical point of view, if all we need is to complete a task, it does not matter if the agent performing such a task was really "intelligent", or if it really understood what was going on and why. All we care about are the result and the success rate.

I realise we have not solved the conundrum of defining intelligence and proving if machines are in fact intelligent or not. But we have shifted our focus to a practical approach, which allows us to evaluate usefulness, not meaning. So bear with me, as we dig into the field of Artificial Intelligence , or the ability of machines to perform "intelligently."

CHAPTER 6

ARTIFICIAL INTELLIGENCE

I have a confession to make. When I chose the title of this book, *Robots Will Steal Your Job*, I was not completely honest with you. Robots will *eventually* steal your job, but before that something else is going to jump in. In fact, it already has, in a much more pervasive way than any physical machine could ever do. I am, of course, talking about computer programs in general. Automated Planning and Scheduling, Machine Learning, Natural Language Processing, Machine Perception, Computer Vision, Speech Recognition, Affective Computing, Computational Creativity, these are all fields of Artificial Intelligence that do not have to contend with the cumbersome issues that Robotics has to face. It is much easier to enhance an algorithm than it is to build a better robot. A more accurate title for this book would have been "*Machine Intelligence and Computer Algorithms Are Already Stealing Your Job, and They Will Do So Ever More in the Future*" – but that was not exactly a catchy title.

The public perceives intelligent machines to be human-like robots that perform our daily duties. Thank you Hollywood! In reality, most "intelligent" agents do not require a physical body, and they operate mostly at the level of computation. Data crunching and aggregation is what they do best. Ironically, it is harder to automate a housemaid than it is to replace a radiologist[31]. A radiologist is a medical doctor who specialises in analysing images generated by various medical scanning technologies. It is a popular area of focus for newly minted doctors, as it offers relatively high pay and regular work hours, there is no need to work on weekends, and there are no emergencies. The downside is that it is a very repetitive job. Even though it takes at least thirteen years of study and training beyond high school, it is quite easy to automate this job[32]. Think about it. The focus of the job is to analyse and evaluate visual images, the parameters of which are well defined since they are often coming directly from computerised scanning devices. It is a closed system, with a number of well-known variables that have mostly already been defined. And the process is very repetitive. What

29

this equates to is a database of information (thirteen years of studies and training) connected to a visual recognition system (the radiologist's brain); a process that already exists today and finds many applications.

Visual pattern recognition software is already highly sophisticated. One such example is Google Images. You can upload an image to the search engine, then Google uses computer vision simulation techniques to match your image to other images in the Google Images index and additional image collections. From those matches, they try to generate an accurate "best guess" text description of your image, as well as find other images that have the same content as your uploaded image.

Figure 6.1: Front page of Google Images. You can see the camera icon on the right of the bar, click that and you can upload your image.

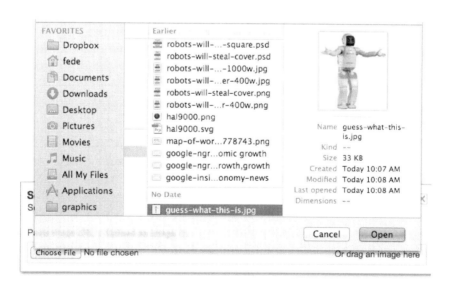

Figure 6.2: I upload my image, named "guess-what-this.is.jpg"

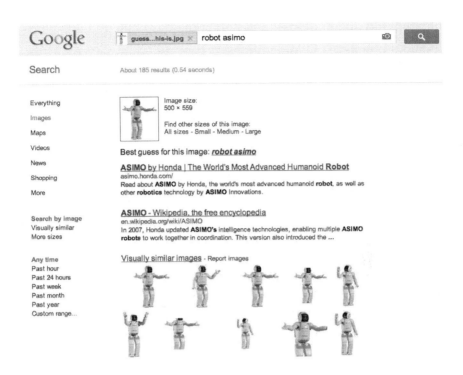

Figure 6.3: The software correctly recognises it as the Robot ASIMO by Honda, and offers similar images in return. Notice that the proposed images show ASIMO in different positions and angles, not the same image in different sizes. This algorithm recognises millions of different patterns, as it is a general-purpose application. A task-specific pattern recognition software is less complex to develop, although it must be much more accurate as the stakes are higher.

Similarly, many governments have access to software that can help identify terrorists in airports based on visual analysis of security photographs[33]. CCTV cameras in London and many other cities have advanced systems that track people's faces and can help the police identify potential criminals[34].

Radiology is already subject to offshoring to India and other places where the average pay for the same task is 10 times as low[35]. How long do you think will pass before we "offshore" to workers that need no pay at all, and all they need is a bit of electricity to run?

In contrast, the duties of a housemaid, a job that requires no education and no particular skills, is a highly complicated set of tasks for a robot. This robot would need sophisticated motor skills and coordination in a 3D environment. It has to recognise thousands of different objects, move freely around the house, do the stairs, apply pressures with extreme care, and make millions of decisions per second; all while consuming very little energy and being cheaper than a $15 per hour housemaid. The most sophisticated robot that could do that is Honda's ASIMO, which costs millions and can't perform as well as a regular housemaid.

Cheap, reliable, human-like robots will eventually be available. But for now, it's AI-time baby!

6.1   SMARTER, BETTER, FASTER, STRONGER

You might think that computers are stupid because they cannot make sense of things like we do. This is true. You can take a toddler, show them a picture, and they will tell you right away if it is a picture of a person, a book or a cat. Computers do not work like that. It is very hard for computer programs to recognise patterns the same way humans do. We can look at pictures, see them in full view and recognise known patterns easily. We are good at this. We have evolved with this unique ability because it gave us an advantage over other species for survival. Computer programs, on the other hand, did not evolve the way our brains did; thus, they work in very different ways. They can do complex mathematical calculations and solve millions of differential equations in one second, whereas many of us struggle to do even the most basic math. Image interpretation, effortless and instantaneous for people, remains a significant challenge for Artificial Intelligence [36]. Computers crunch data, while we make sense of it all. This has been true for quite some time, but is it still the case today?

Recent developments in the field of Artificial Intelligence , specifically Machine Learning applications, have begun to change this. Over the last 20 years, we have devised and perfected various mathematical algorithms that can learn from experience, just as we do. The principle behind them is quite simple: train a computer program to learn, without explicitly programming it. How does that work? There are various methods to achieve this: supervised and unsupervised learning, reinforcement learning, transduction, with several variations and combinations of them. Each of these methods then apply specific algorithms, some of which you may be aware of (e.g. neural networks), and most of which probably sound very obscure (e.g. support vector machines, linear regression, naive Bayes). You do not need to learn the specifics, but the main idea is this: just as we learn through experience, so do these programs. They have evolved.

We might not be so different from them after all.

6.2   IT'S ALL ABOUT THE ALGORITHMS

Learning algorithms are improving in terms of accuracy and performance every day. Just five or six years ago they were very sloppy and their results were invalid. Today, however, things are changing rapidly. Google search results used to be the same for everyone, no matter where you came from. Today, it is likely that no Google search ever gives the exact same results. Instead, what you get is a personalised version, containing the pages that are most likely to interest you, based on a variety of criteria. Say you search for a Pizzeria. They can look at your IP address, they can geolocate you using GPS technology, and return the top results in your area. If you have a registered Google account, they can look at the history of all your previous searches, where you clicked, when you clicked, how many times, which domain you visited the most (or the least). They know if you are male or female, young or old, and based on that they can narrow down the search to an even more personalised level. If you have a Gmail account, they will know many things about your habits, the places you visit, the places you wish to visit, and the people you usually talk to. They can cross-reference their searches and use that data as well. Of course, when I say "they", I do not mean any particular person. There is nobody personally looking at your profile, your data, your search history, or your habits. That would violate privacy laws. I mean the programs. All that I have described happens billions of times a day, in a matter of milliseconds or less, for each occurrence. Beside the fact that having a person check on you like that would violate privacy laws, it would also be practically impossible to do these operations with human supervision. But every day these programs learn something new about us.

Another major difference is that computers can learn faster and have virtually no limitation on how much they can learn (due to the exponential increase in computational power and in memory storage, respectively). Think about it: it takes a few years to teach a child to learn a language, read, write, recognise things, and even more time to learn a sophisticated technical skill. To become a qualified medical doctor, it can take 20+ years of studying and experience before becoming proficient. If one day that doctor dies, simply stops working, goes on permanent vacation or retires, it will take another 20 years for the next person to take their place. Granted, the entire profession might advance, but the time required to get up-to-speed with current standards does not change much. Computers do not have such limitations. It might require a lot of time at the beginning, but once any progress is made it is propagated throughout the whole network. The next computer does not need to re-learn everything from scratch – it can simply connect to the existing network and benefit from the collective knowledge gained by the contributions of other computers.

Sure, the algorithm used is important. If you have a bad algorithm, you will end up with nothing interesting. But what has really made the most difference in the last 10 years is the sheer volume of data at our disposal. We are literally buried by data of all kinds, so much so that we do not have enough minds to analyse that data and make sense of it all. Over the last few years there has been a wave of public data coming from all sources: governments, NGOs, public libraries, as well as private websites that collect real-time data from people. We contribute in creating this immense database of collective knowledge, simply by living our lives. Every tweet we transmit, search we generate, picture we upload, friend we add on a social network, place we visit, phone call we make, all feed this massive distributed super-computer that is composed of the billions of computers around the globe that are connected to each other through the Internet.

That said, you might be wondering how far we have come with AI Systems. Have they reached human-level intelligence? If not, will they ever? What technology exists already?

For now you can rest safe. AI systems have not come anywhere near human levels of *general purpose intelligence*. However, they are evolving rapidly, and some expect them to reach and even surpass humans by 2030.[37] Others disagree, and only time will tell for sure who is right.

What we know for certain is that today we *already* have machines that surpass humans in many *task-specific intelligences*. This leads us next into exploring the evidence of automation.

CHAPTER 7

EVIDENCE OF AUTOMATION

We understand what exponential growth means. We have seen how information technology has grown over the last 150 years. Let us see how far has that brought us.

I started gathering the evidence for this chapter as soon as I decided to write the book in October 2011. Since then, I have collected more than 300 articles, all from reputable and reliable sources. These stories cover machines that act like us, computers that "think" better than us, and robots that perform unimaginably complex tasks. Every day I opened my news feed to find something new and then added it to my list. At a certain point I realised I had to stop. I knew there could never be an end to this trend, but I did not expect it to grow so quickly. Once again, I underestimated the power of the exponential function. As the list started to grow out of proportion, I decided I would freeze it, finish the book, and publish, or else I would never finish it. To offer readers a current resource, I will continue to post updates on the website http://robotswillstealyourjob.com. In this book, rather than offering a long and sterile list of technologies, I will discuss only a few that I think are the most relevant for the sake of the argument.

7.1   AUTOMATED SHOPPING

You might not think of them as such, but vending machines are actually a primitive type of robot. Their function is very simple. They keep an inventory, have an electronic display, accept money, and provide you with the item you purchased. It is a 30-year-old technology and it has not progressed much since then. Or, has it? In Europe and the US we do not think much of vending machines, but that is just because we have not taken them seriously. In Japan, however, where they have high population density, limited space, high cost of labour, low rates of vandalism and petty crimes, and people shop mostly by bicycle or on foot, vending machines are taken very seriously.

In Japan there are about 8.6 million vending machines, one for every 14 people, the highest number pro capita in the world.[38]. These robots, known there as ????? (jid?-hanbaiki) from jid?, or "automatic"; hanbai, or "vending"; and ki, or "machine", often abbreviated ??? (jihanki), are widespread and commonly used for all sorts of goods: not just newspapers, snacks, and drinks, but also books, DVDs, condoms, ice-cream, hot instant noodles, rice, magazines, glasses, boiled eggs, umbrellas, neck ties, sneakers, vegetables, iPods, live lobsters, Onsen (hot spring water), and even Buddhist prayer bead-rolls. Sure, we can laugh at it, but doesn't it make sense? The days when you had the little shop just around the corner – with a smiling person who owned the shop, knew what they were doing, and could give you real guidance and assistance – are quickly disappearing.

Most commercial transactions of physical goods today are made at the mall and huge supermarket chains. The cashiers at these companies work part-time, as one of the multiple jobs they hold because just one job will not provide the money they need to pay their rent, medical bills, student loads, mortgages, etc. The truth is that it would make a whole lot of sense for society to have a shopping mall where most things are automated. The problem with that, of course, is that people currently working there would find themselves in deep, deep trouble.

Imagine this. You walk into a store and you have an interactive map on your cell phone showing you where all the items are. You can search for items, filter them by categories, and get information on each single product that goes far beyond nutrition facts; you can trace the production process, the companies behind it, and dynamically compare products based on your search criteria. You can also read reviews from other people about these products, just like on Amazon.com today. Before leaving with your items, you stop for a few seconds in an assessment zone that receives signals from RFID chips in the merchandise. Then you swipe your credit card, or just accept the payment request on your cell phone. The whole process, the time between when you decide to leave the store and the moment you can actually walk out, takes less than 10 seconds. No human was involved in this, no human was required. No queues, no waiting time.

Sound futuristic? Every piece of technology needed to make this happen already exists, and has existed for many years. Then why is it not in place already? Why are we not seeing this trend expanding to all retail stores? Maybe it is expensive to deploy such a system. Actually, it would be much cheaper than having to employ humans to do the job. "But you need human contact! What about the value added that only a human employee can offer?" Have you ever worked at a mall? If so, how motivated were you and how long did that last? "But you need human workers to place the products on the shelves!" Actually, even that technology is already available, though it is more recent than the others. Some warehouses are already completely automated, and require only operators to work and handle the entire task. Pallets and product move on a system of automated conveyors, cranes, and automated storage and retrieval systems coordinated by programmable logic controllers and computers running logistics automation software. Their accuracy and productivity far exceeds that produced by human labour. These machines are faster and more precise, they can lift huge weights without having to deal with back problems, they work day and night, and do not require much maintenance. Amazon.com recently made a $775 million purchase of Kiva Systems, a manufacturer of bright orange robots that scuttle around warehouses filling orders[39]. CNN has a video of the system operating (see the link in the previous footnote or the book website). It is a pretty amazing sight. Hundreds of robots transporting merchandise around immense warehouses, with clockwork precision and perfect timing, as if dancing to a silent piece of music written in code of zeroes and ones. These robots are smart enough to put the items in the most convenient place and distance, based on how frequently they are needed, how heavy they are, and many other criteria. They work 24/7 and never make mistakes. The application of similar automated systems to supermarkets and shopping malls is a minor engineering issue, one that can easily be solved in a few months, if there was ever the intention to do so.

If this is all possible, why are we not seeing it?

Tesco is the third-largest retailer in the world measured by revenues (after Walmart and Carrefour) and the second-largest measured by profits (after Walmart). Tesco has a large market in South Korea (where they are branded as "Home plus"), second only to E-Mart mainly because that company has more stores. As one might expect, they wanted to increase profits. The typical approach would require them to build more stores in order to reach E-marts level of distribution in the country. They opted for a different strategy, one that uses more automation and less workers.

Picture yourself in Korea going to work. You need a few things for dinner, but don't have much time. While waiting for the next subway train to arrive, you see the walls covered with displays that look like supermarket shelves. You use your cell phone to scan the QR code on the items you want and then check out. When you get home, you will find your groceries have been delivered to your doorstep. Quite convenient, isn't it? The results of this experiment are in: online sales between November 2010 and January 2011 increased by 130%, with the number of registered members rising by 76%. Home plus had become the number one online store, while successfully raising the stakes in the offline market[40].

This continuing trend could potentially destabilise the economy. Consider the millions of employed who would be affected by it. If Walmart were to put this technology in place on a systemic level (automated restocking, shopping, and delivery), the consequences to those currently employed by them would be disastrous. It would be practically impossible for most of them to find another job. The average person does not realise how big Walmart really is. Today, Walmart is the largest retailer on the planet. In fact, it is much more than that: the finances, footprint, and personnel of this behemoth dwarf entire industries and countries[41]. Its epic $421 billion annual revenues eclipse the GDP of more than 170 countries. Its 2.1 million employees could form the second largest standing army on the planet. Walmart's 2010 revenues were bigger than the revenues of the largest oil companies, the largest manufacturer, and the largest pharmaceutical company in the United States. Even when combined, the revenues of Chevron, General Electric, and Pfizer still total less than Walmart's. To put this in perspective, if Walmart were a country, its GDP would be the 25th largest economy in the world (twice the size of Ireland's). If Walmart were to initiate an aggressive automation strategy, in just a few years it could easily run its business with less than 100,000 employees. That would leave 2 million people, mostly uneducated and unskilled workers, out of a job. Where would these people go? And what would they eat? What will happen to their families?

In the past, we have seen automation cutting the workforce, but unskilled workers all gravitated towards places like Walmart to find an easy (although very unsatisfying) job. *This is one of many unspoken tragedies of the so-called modern culture. The idea that the greatest aspiration a person could have is to work some mechanical and monotonous job, so that they can pay the bills, is an insult to the dignity of every individual. Each human being, from the moment they are born, is an invaluable masterpiece, capable of greatness beyond what we can conceive today. To even consider the proposition that we should hang on to an economic system that hinders innovation and automation, in order to preserve repetitive and mindless jobs, shows the deep loss of perspective and aptitude of our out-dated institutions.*

If Walmart begins automation (and I suspect they will), there would be no coming back for the shopping industry. It is an irreversible process. The replaced jobs will not come back. But having removed these jobs, what will millions of people do?

Wait before you answer, we are not quite done yet.

7.2   AUTOMATED MANUFACTURING

The advent of automation in the manufacturing industry is generally well-known. It has been a century since we started using machines to increase our productivity. Just think of a car factory. The assembly line developed by Ford Motor Company between 1908 and 1915 made automated assembly widespread and mass production brought unprecedented social transformations. By reinterpreting the old Latin proverb *divide et impera* (divide and conquer), we were able to transform long and difficult tasks into sets of many small and simple-to-execute mechanical operations. This approach worked well with machines which, for a century, integrated with humans in fruitful cooperation.

Robots were displacing human workers, but we always found something else to do, because of mainly two reasons:

- There was enough time to adjust and learn new skills.

- Some operations were too complex for machines to do, or the cost of creating a machine capable of performing such a task was too high. Why go through the trouble of programming a complex robot to do something cheap labour could accomplish more easily and at less cost?

Such was the past, but things are different now. Labour is no longer so cheap. Human development is finally occurring on a mass scale.People are (justifiably) demanding their rights. Even though there are still millions who work in conditions that we might consider slavery by today's standards, the working conditions and standards are raising everywhere, even in relatively under-developed countries. On the other hand algorithms are improving exponentially, robotics technology is developing rapidly, and machines are now becoming cheaper to build (even for complex tasks). We are already seeing the effects of this everywhere.

Foxconn is the largest maker of electronic components in the world and the largest exporter in Greater China,[42,43] with an annual revenue of more than 100 billion dollars.[44] They can make virtually anything. If you have an iPad, an iPhone, a Kindle, a PlayStation 3 or an Xbox 360, chances are high that Foxconn made it. Without counting national public services, Foxconn comes out as the third largest employer in the world with an impressive 1.2 million workers, right after Walmart (2.1 million).[45] It has contracts with Acer, Amazon.com, Apple, Cisco, Dell, Hewlett-Packard, Intel, Microsoft, Motorola, Nintendo, Nokia, Samsung, Sony, Toshiba, and just about any major tech company you can think of. Foxconn is not a company: it is an immense monster, an electronics supergiant that is singlehandedly responsible for nearly half of all such technological production in the world.[46]

If they were to displace their 1.2 million workers, things would turn ugly for many people. As it happens, as recently as last year (2011), Foxconn said that they intended to deploy an army of robots in order to "replace some of its workers with 1 million robots in three years to cut rising labor expenses and improve efficiency." – as announced by Terry Gou, founder and chairman of the company.[47] It still remains unclear if they are really going through with the plan, and how many workers would be displaced by this initiative, but it appears that they have already launched and built a Research and Development facility and a factory in Taiwan to build their own robots; and have begun to hire some 2,000 engineers to drive the project forward.[48] It appears that Foxconn is committed to the automation of their business, and it should come as no surprise. Why wouldn't they? Robots are cheaper and more reliable than human workers, they do not ask for vacation, they do not commit suicide, they do not protest for more rights, and they can ensure the company's profits – which is what matters most for a multinational corporation and its stakeholders.

Rumors and stories surrounding Foxconn's operations began to spread after a wave of suicides was reported by the news in the Western world. After fourteen workers were found dead in 2010, some twenty Chinese universities compiled a report in which they described Foxconn factories as labour camps and detailed widespread worker abuse and illegal overtime.[49] Stories of overcrowding, tiny living accommodations, impossibly long and exhausting work hours, and security guards beating workers to death are just hints of what happens in those hellholes, from what manages to overcome the great firewall of censorship in China to reach our digital shores.[50] After protests began to kindle in the US and in Europe, demanding better working conditions, the morbid response from Foxconn executives was that they would install suicide-prevention nets at some facilities to catch the people who tried to commit suicide by jumping off the building (I am not joking), and they promised to offer higher wages at its Shenzhen production bases. But they also did something else. Workers are now forced to sign a legally binding document guaranteeing that they and their descendants will not sue the company in the event of unexpected death, self-injury, or suicide.[51]

The saddest part of this story is not the that workers at Foxconn live in horrifying conditions. What is truly astonishing is that Foxconn actually provides higher wages, better working conditions, and has a lower suicide rate than the average Chinese company.[52] Foxconn is merely the story that made it into the news that we suddenly became all outraged by. But there is nothing to be surprised about: this is the very nature of our current socio-economic system, *efficiency and, consequently, profits are considered more important than human lives.*

Foxconn is not the only company moving in the direction of automation. **Canon** announced in June 2012 that some of its camera factories will phase out human workers in an effort to reduce costs. We can expect robots to be making the next generation of cameras, possibly as soon as 2015. Of course, the company's spokesman Jun Misumi was quick at dismissing the idea that this move would mean layoffs at Canon when he told the Associated Press, "When machines become more sophisticated, human beings can be transferred to do new kinds of work".[53] These are nice words, but I doubt they will hold true. Assembly line workers have been performing the same mindless, repetitive, mechanical jobs for years. Before they started working at a factory they were masterpieces of evolution and natural selection, individuals with imagination, dreams, and aspirations. They had endless possibilities. They could have become artists, scientists, and musicians. They could have been the drivers of new amazing discoveries that pushed humanity forward. After a few years in a factory they each became just another pair of hands in an endless sea of moving parts, their dreams were crushed; their hopes and aspirations reduced merely to bringing home just enough to keep their heads above water for another month. I doubt these people will all suddenly become engineers, industrial designers, sales managers, and computer scientists – if we imagine that a proportionally larger number of those jobs might be needed at Canon in 2015 (they will not be).

Foxconnn and Canon are only two of numerous examples. China is increasingly replacing its workers with robots [54] and now even major newspapers are realising this. Just a few days ago (at the time of writing), The New York Times came out with a 6-page piece titled "The Machines Are Taking Over"[55] and The Wall Street Journal says "Why Software Is Eating The World".[56] I suspect these types of articles will only increase in the near future.

The trend is clear. Companies in the manufacturing sector are automating and the typical statement that "people will find something else to do" is simply a cop-out that does not look at the reality of the situation – that change is happening too fast and that most workers who will be replaced by machines will not have the time to learn new skills. Assuming, of course, that we could somehow find a number of new jobs equivalent to the number of displaced workers – I very much doubt we will (more on this in Chapter 9).

7.3 3D PRINTING

You are in your house having a party with some friends. As it happens, one of them drinks a little bit too much and drops a glass on the floor. Typically you would have to go out and buy a new one, or get online and order it. But, you could also go the computer, download the CAD file of the glass, press print, and watch your 3D printer as it makes a perfect replica of the glass to replace the one your friend broke. Pretty neat, but not really a game changer.

Now imagine you are Captain of a container ship. You left from China a few days ago on your way to San Francisco and now you are in the middle of the Pacific Ocean. Suddenly the ship stops and the Chief Engineer comes to the bridge to tell you that a part of the engine just broke. He does not have a spare part and has no way of making a replacement. You realise you are stranded. All you can do is call for help, wait, miss the deadline, and lose a lot of money. Not a pretty situation. Or, you could have a 3D printer. Select the file, press print, fix the engine, and be on your way in less than an hour. *That* is pretty neat.

It?s like the replicator in Star Trek[57]. "Tea. Earl Grey. Hot." Many fans of The Next Generation will recognise these words. Just say the word and anything you want will appear right in front of your eyes. How far are we from this fantastic technology?

Figure 7.1: The replicator in Star Trek creating a coffee mug.

Today 3D printing is a multi-billion dollar industry, and it is growing exponentially[58]. There are many types of 3D printer, from DIY Open Source models to sophisticated commercial products, spanning from a few hundred to many thousands of dollars. The idea behind it is simple. Just like regular inkjet or laser printers, they start from a file on your computer and then manipulate matter to create what you want. The only difference is that they can print in three dimensions instead of two, and they can use many different materials. 3D printers are already used for rapid prototyping, rapid manufacturing, and many DIY enthusiasts and hackers use them at home for fun. Although these machines are not quite ready to replace all commercial production, they surely are on their way. The hugely successful Open Source project RepRap gave rise to a plethora of successors, thanks to its openness and the incredible community of people around it. Just to name of few of the available 3D printers under €1,000, we have MakerBot Thing-O-Matic, The Replicator, Ultimaker, Shapercube, Mosaic, Prusa, Huxley, Printrbot. They all came into existence in just a couple of years, and if you buy it in kit form and assemble it yourself, you can get one for less than

€300.

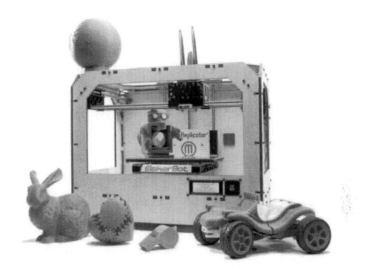

Figure 7.2: The "Replicator", an inexpensive 3D printer that prints object in colours.

Printers in the lower price range are still very limited, both in terms of resolution (you can see the imperfections) and the materials they can use (mostly plastics). However, commercial printers are different. At the time of this writing, the most sophisticated machine can print with an accuracy of 16 micrometres[59]. That's 0.016 millimetres! To put things in perspective, the resolution limit of the human eye is about 100 micrometres, and the iPhone 4's 'Retina display' pixels are 78 micrometres in width[60]. These machines can print multiple materials, such as ABS plastic, PLA, polyamide (nylon), glass filled polyamide, stereolithography materials (epoxy resins), silver, titanium, wax, polystyrene, ceramics, stainless steel, titanium, photopolymers, polycarbonate, aluminium and various alloys including cobalt chrome.[61] You can print in colour and even create structures that are more intricate than any other manufacturing technology – or, in fact, are impossible to build in any other way.[62] You can create parts with moving components, hinges, and even parts within parts.

3D printers are not just used as an alternative to standard manufacturing. People have printed really cool-looking personalised prosthetic limbs,[63] bone-like material,[64] and even human organs.[65] [66]

A very inspiring example of how 3D printers can be used for the betterment of humankind comes from Scott Summit and his team composed of Industrial Designers and Orthopaedic Surgeons, whose mission is to provide a sensitive and

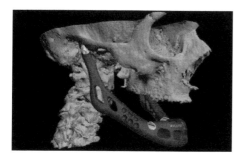 

Figure 7.3: A 3D printer-created lower jaw that has been fitted to an 83-year-old woman's face in what doctors say is the first operation of its kind.

personalised service to people who have congenital or traumatic limb loss. In their words: "Each of our bodies is unique, as are our tastes and styles. Humans are anything but one-size-fits-all, and we want to recognise that fact. We achieve this by creating products that allow our clients to personalise their prosthetic legs. Our hope is to enable our clients to emotionally connect with their prosthetic limbs, and wear them confidently as a form of personal expression."[67] For people who have lost a leg, life can be very difficult. So, instead of hiding their defect and feeling ashamed of it, they can show their personalised prosthetic leg with pride, thereby reclaiming that lost connection with their body.

I expect we will soon see a rapid increase in the quality of these machines, with the costs dropping so significantly that they will become an everyday commodity, like a microwave oven, and will be found in most houses. Marketplaces like iTunes, Android, and Amazon.com will follow, along with their 'pirate' and Open Source counterparts. In fact, the Open Source community is already leading the way (as always). Thingiverse has thousands of free designs that people can download, print, or improve upon,[68] and The Pirate Bay recently announced a new section called "Physible," CAD designs of physical objects, legal or not[69]. In a few years, most of us will all have a micrometre-precision 3D printer that prints multiple materials and colours in our house. Designs will be extremely cheap, or cost nothing at all.

Today 3D printing is little more than a hobby, but it will probably soon become a game changer for entire industries. Another advantage of 3D printing is that instead of conforming to sizes and shapes defined by the economies of scale, the object can adapt to you, instead, moving from an economy of mass production to an economy of mass personalisation. How many jobs today rely on manufacturing? We'll probably see them disappear, too.

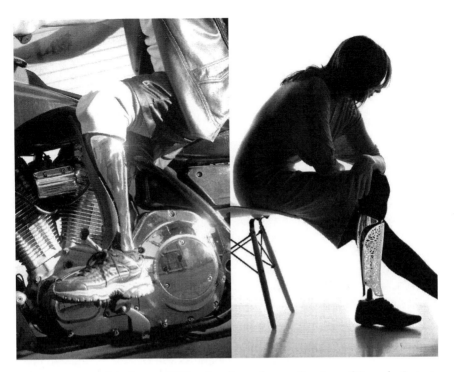

Figure 7.4: Beautiful pictures of 3D printed prostheses. Courtesy of Bespoke Innovations™, Inc.

7.4 AUTOMATED CONSTRUCTION

Typically, it can take from 6 weeks to 6 months to build a 2-storey house in the US or Canada, mostly because dozens of humans do all the work. However, we have newer and smarter ways of building houses, which some are beginning to use. In China, they can construct a 30-storey skyscraper with all modern comforts in 15 days. That's 2 storeys per day, non-stop. The building is made from prefabricated parts and can withstand earthquakes of magnitude 9. It has excellent insulation systems, is five times more efficient than regular hotels, and has smart systems for air circulation and quality control[70]. The implications of this are significant: we have designed a system that will let you build anywhere, to construction tolerances of +/- 0.2 mm, in just a few days[71].

This is what we can do today. Let us have a look at tomorrow, shall we?

Contour crafting is a construction process that uses a computer-controlled crane or gantry to construct buildings rapidly and efficiently without manual labour. It is possible that within a decade this technology will advance so much that we will be able to upload the design specifications to our computer, press print, and watch massive robots spit out a concrete house in less than a day. No humans required, except for a few supervisors and designers. You might be thinking this is like a huge 3D printer! And you would be right. The idea is the same, only the scale and the materials differ.

Contour crafting is now under development by Behrokh Khoshnevis of the University of Southern California's Information Sciences Institute. It was originally conceived as a method to construct moulds for industrial parts, but Khoshnevis decided to adapt the technology for rapid home construction as a way to rebuild after natural disasters like the devastating earthquakes that have plagued his native Iran.[72] Khoshnevis claims that his system could build a complete home in a single day, and its electrically powered crane would produce very little construction material waste. This is particularly interesting because today a standard home construction project creates 3 to 7 tonnes of waste, as well as exhaust fumes from machinery and vehicles,[73] not to mention the thousands of deaths each year which result from workplace accidents.[74] Contour crafting could reduce costs, lessen our environmental impact, and save materials and lives. Of course, many jobs would disappear, too.

Some industries and institutions have already shown interest in this technology. Caterpillar, Inc. has provided funding for the Viterbi project since the summer of 2008,[75] NASA is evaluating Contour Crafting for its application in the construction of bases on Mars and the Moon,[76] and Singularity University graduate students established the ACASA project with Khoshnevis as the CTO to commercialise Contour Crafting.[77]

7.5   AUTOMATED JOURNALISM

You might think that writing is one of those things that machines will never do. Sure you can program them to generate text, but it will sound sterile and fake. It would have no soul. You would be able to spot it in a second, right? Right?

Let us see how well you do. Below are the opening lines of three story pieces written about a baseball game. Can you tell which were written by flesh-and-blood humans, and which (if any) were written by a computer?

a) *The University of Michigan baseball team used a four-run fifth inning to salvage the final game in its three-game weekend series with Iowa, winning 7-5 on Saturday afternoon (April 24) at the Wilpon Baseball Complex, home of historic Ray Fisher Stadium.*

b) *Michigan held off Iowa for a 7-5 win on Saturday. The Hawkeyes (16-21) were unable to overcome a four-run sixth inning deficit.*

The Hawkeyes clawed back in the eighth inning, putting up one run.

c) *The Iowa baseball team dropped the finale of a three-game series, 7-5, to Michigan Saturday afternoon. Despite the loss, Iowa won the series having picked up two wins in the twinbill at Ray Fisher Stadium Friday.*

Take a moment and try to guess. They all look pretty similar, but which one is the product of a lifeless machine? All of them? None? It is time for the moment of truth. If you thought article c) was computer generated, then you would be right. I can picture you going back a paragraph and read the opening lines again thinking, "Yeah, now that I see it, it makes sense. None of them are Pulitzer Prize material, but c) definitely looks more dull than the others. It must be computer generated". Somehow your mind has already internalised this fact, and it is starting to reinforce it. If you go back and read them again, I am sure you can spot the flaw right away. As with subliminal messages, once you are aware of them, they don?t work any more.

Sorry to disappoint, but you have just been *trolled.*[78] The correct answer is in fact b), *that* is the computer generated article.[79] If you fell for the trick, don?t feel too bad. Narrative Science and other companies have many customers in the big media industry that make use of this technology already. Most people just don?t notice. The identity of these media firms is secret, but we know they are there because the companies that created these intelligent algorithms have earned several million dollars in a very short time. This software is currently mainly used for sports, finance, business, market, and real estate reporting. I will not go so far as to say that the algorithms developed today can replace all journalists. And I do not expect software to write an editorial about the lack of human rights in China any time soon. But remember, to disrupt an industry you do not need to replace *all* jobs within it, just a significant fraction.

I have noticed that often people tend to express some form of the following logical fallacy: *If you can find one example of a person that cannot be replaced by machines, then the argument of technological unemployment is invalid.* On the contrary, I would argue that if you have to rely on that single special example to present your argument in favour of humans, you have just proved my point. The average person within that job type is bound to fall victim to technological unemployment.

Now, just imagine if a few of the big players (e.g. Google, Amazon.com, etc.) that are collecting millions of terabytes of personal information about our reading habits decide to enter the market of automated journalism. We have already seen how Google news has affected news sites by collecting articles into categories and creating personalised news feeds faster and better than any human can. What if these types of software start to write the stories themselves? How long do you think will that take? If you are thinking decades, you are in for a surprise.

7.6   AI ASSISTANTS

You might remember May of 1997, when the legendary chess player Garry Kasparov was defeated by IBM Deep Blue in what has been called "the most spectacular chess event in history."[80] At the time, the plan of IBM was to rely on the computational superiority of their machine using *brute force*,[81] crunching billions of combinations; against the intuition, memory recall, and pattern recognition of the Russian chess grandmaster. Nobody believed it represented an act of intelligence of any sort, since it worked in a very mechanistic way. Boy, have we come so far since then.

The classic "Turing test approach" has been largely abandoned as a realistic research goal, and is now just an intellectual curiosity (the annual Loebner prize for realistic chattiest[82]), but helped spawn the two dominant themes of modern cognition and artificial intelligence: calculating probabilities and producing complex behaviour from the interaction of many small, simple processes. As of today (2012), we believe these replicate more closely what the human brain does, and they have been used in a variety of real-world applications: Google's autonomous cars, search results, recommendation systems, automated language translation, personal assistants, cybernetic computational search engines, and IBM's newest super brain **Watson**.

Natural language processing was believed to be a task that only humans could accomplish. A word can have different meanings depending on the context, a phrase doesn?t mean what it says if it is a joke or a pun. One may infer an implicit subtext or make cultural references specific to a geographical or cultural area. The possibilities are truly endless. A game that captures pretty well the intricacies and the nuances of the English language is *Jeopardy!* This show that has been on-the-air for half a century and has showcased some remarkable geniuses. Brad Rutter is the biggest all-time winner on the game (making $3,455,102 so far[83]) and Ken Jennings is the record holder for the longest championship streak (74 wins[84]).

In February 2011, IBM's team decided to take on both champions in a historic match between humans and machine. It was the moment of truth. Watson dominated both humans, bringing home the prize of $1 million (which was donated to charities), while Jennings and Rutter received $300,000 and $200,000, respectively, with both pledging to donate half their winnings to charity. This was a truly historic moment for AI researchers because they were able to reach a frontier that only science fiction writers and futurists believed was possible just a few years ago.

Although IBM's achievement is impressive, we have to put things in perspective. Watson had access to 200 million pages of structured and unstructured content, consuming four terabytes of disk storage, including the full text of Wikipedia. The hardware is a 2,880 processor cores monster, running on massive parallelism that allows Watson to answer *Jeopardy!* questions in less than three seconds.[85] The total cost of the hardware is about $3 million. Watson's brain uses 80 kilowatts of electricity and 20 air conditioners,[86] while Ken Jennings and Brad Rutter's brains fit in a shoebox and are powered by a couple glasses of water and a few sandwiches.

Now, I invite you to recall the power of exponential growth in computing. While our brains will remain relatively unchanged for the next 20 years, computer efficiency and computational power will have doubled about twenty times. That is a million-fold increase. So, for the same $3 million you will have a computer a million times more powerful than Watson, or you could have a Watson-equivalent computer for $3.

Watson's computational power and exceptional skills of advanced Natural Language Processing, Information Retrieval, Knowledge Representation and Reasoning, Machine Learning, and open domain question answering are already being put to better use than showing off at a TV contest. IBM and Nuance Communications, Inc. are partnering for the research project to develop a commercial product during the next 18 to 24 months that will exploit Watson's capabilities as a clinical decision support system to aid the diagnosis and treatment of patients.[87] Recall the example of automated radiologists we mentioned earlier. Watson could be fully capable of performing this task if there was ever the intention of doing so, and even then we would be using only a tiny fraction of its immense power.

This is just the beginning. Watson-like technologies could be used for virtually anything: legal advice, city planning (IBM and Cisco are already working on smart cities),[88] and why not policy-making?[89]

The Internet of Things is coming and we had better be ready. Technology is becoming so cheap and so powerful it will be integrated into everyday objects, which will help us make better decisions. With all objects in the world equipped with minuscule identifying devices, daily life on Earth would undergo a transformation of epic proportions.[90] Companies would not run out of stock, nor would they waste products, since involved parties would know which products are required and consumed.[91] Mislaid and stolen items would be easily tracked and located, as would the people who use them. Your ability to interact with objects could be altered remotely based on your current status and existing user agreements. We are not quite there yet, but we are getting closer and closer.[92]

Coming back to the present, let us see what the market has to offer today. Siri is Apple's attempt to create a personal assistant, and anyone who has ever used it knows that it is little more than a toy. Anybody trying to convince you otherwise is talking marketing trash. Right now it has some built-in AI to recognise speech and create a few connections in the dialogue, make appointments, and send emails; then it queries the computation search engine WolframAlpha to give you computer results to natural language questions; but it does not go very far. The so-called 'smart-assistant' understands very little of natural language, it does not adapt to many different accents, and it feels nothing like talking to a real person. Generally speaking, it feels like you have to adapt to it, rather than vice versa.

That being said, one cannot overlook its immense potential, given what we learned in the chapter *Information Technology* about the power of the exponential curve. Siri is just the first prototype of a soon-to-be truly smart-assistant that understands any language, spoken by anybody, and helps them with whatever need they might have. In time, it will evolve more and more, becoming increasingly intelligent (meaning useful, not necessarily 'intelligent' as we are). Its progress will be automatically propagated to all the connected devices, anywhere in the world, instantly. Google is already working on a competitor for Siri as part of its Android platform, and we can expect IBM's Watson to play a role in the scene as well. And these are just the known players. Today, a team of 3 to 4 people with access to cloud computing can create a revolutionary new intelligent system that can be used by millions of people. The initial investment is very low and the distributed nature of computation allows costs to increase incrementally as the business expands.

We are about to experience tremendous changes in such technologies, the consequences of which are unimaginable for us at the moment. Just as cavemen could not imagine the complex cities and societies we live in today, neither can we anticipate in any accurate detail what is soon to come.

7.7   AUTONOMOUS VEHICLES

-People often say that something is either obvious and everything will change, or that it will never happen. It turns out things are not quite that simple. Societies are multi-faceted, complex, evolving organisms, with many variables, and a certain degree of unpredictability. Technicians often fail to take into account the human factor, the psychology of the masses, and how events unfold naturally. I think that both perspectives do not really capture the essence of how we, as people, respond to these events. Humanists do not usually understand technology, so their social critique falls short in the face of disruptive change.

Suppose we take the case of automated vehicles. These are self-driving machines: cars, trucks, and buses that do not require a human driver. The idea of self-driving vehicles has been around for a while in popular culture, thanks to science fiction writers. But for the first time, we have the engineering, the mathematical and the computational ability to transform this idea into reality. Some people are enthusiastic about this technology. "It's about time. I cannot wait to finally get one of those" - said one of the people I interviewed - "It is pretty obvious that human drivers are going to disappear very soon". But I also received very different answers: "I don't trust machines, they'll never be like us. I will never get into a car like that, I want to have control. People won't accept that, they'll never have automated cars running on the streets." This vision is shared by many others I interviewed, some of whom were particularly disturbed by the idea of self-driving cars (surprisingly enough, even young people).

There are many factors to consider, and the evolution of progress goes through various steps. First, there is the development of a new technology. Computer scientists, mathematicians, physicists, and engineers form a small research team somewhere, and decide they want to tackle a specific problem. After a few years of research and development, sometimes even just a few months, they have a working prototype. They test it, improve it, and test it again. They change the conditions, and test it again, and again, until they are satisfied with the result. Now, we have a working technology that has been thoroughly stress-tested under normal as well as extreme conditions, and all the data suggests that this technology is reliable. In fact, it is more reliable than any human; it is safer to use and faster to operate. This represents just the first step. Next comes the social acceptance of such technology. This is not as straightforward as it might seem. Remember that people react very differently to the idea of utilising these machines. Most of the time contrasting opinions are caused by a lack of understanding of the basics of the technology in question. They see it as a matter of trust, or belief. They form their opinion based on intuition, or gut feeling. Whatever the case may be, these different stances are real, and have very serious consequences. As a result, just because a technology exists and it helps us live better, it will not necessarily be adopted right away because of many social factors.

To explain how this process unfolds, I will try to predict what I think is a possible future scenario for the case of self-driving cars. Needless to say, I do not possess the power of precognition, but I will try to make an educated guess. Some of these events, at the time of writing, have already happened. Many have not. Time will tell if I was right or wrong.

7.8   A (POSSIBLE) HISTORY OF SELF-DRIVING CARS

Google announced that they have invented self-driving cars. After a few years of research, with very little money, and a small team, they were able to harness the power of machines to solve a very challenging problem of our times. By utilising neural networks and other sophisticated machine-learning algorithms, an immense quantity of data, and thanks to the power of exponentially-increasing technologies that made computation cheaper and faster, as well as sensors, GPS, and laser systems, Google now had a working prototype of a car that drives without the need for a human driver. They then began to test the car on the streets, and let it run for thousands of kilometres. It recognised street signs, traffic lights, pedestrians, dogs crossing, everything around it. It had a 360-degree vision of the surrounding area. It could operate under any conditions, including sun, rain, fog, icy roads, snow, large roads, and small roads. It could travel across the countryside, along highways, and through traffic-intense cities, all while avoiding obstacles. It even prevented accidents from happening when a potentially dangerous event popped-up, such as a child jumping into the middle of the road, or a bicycle moving towards the centre-line without any warning – situations that had, of course, been anticipated by the design team. They then announced these results to the public. People were divided and picked sides quite easily on the spot. Most of them did not bother to investigate: they either loved it or hated it *a priori*. The media did not help either, as many news anchors discarded the whole thing with a few uninformed remarks; and the public did not receive any information that might change their minds. Since the very reason they watched the news was to become informed, they accepted what they heard at face-value. Some news channels provided a very good service; but far too often they simply gave personal opinions, coming from somebody who had no understanding of the subject and who was paid by the network to display their ignorance and propagate it to the audience.

Meanwhile, further tests were performed and the cars began to gather the attention of many companies and investors. They planned to release the first versions of hybrids, partially-automated vehicles, where the default option is human-driving, but one can switch to automated at any time, and let the car drive for itself. A few states and countries proposed new laws that regulated these cars, and insurance companies made plans to adjust their policies accordingly. This process took some time – months, and in some cases even years, mostly because of the social tensions that began to emerge. The central issue was safety and responsibility: what if an accident happens, who is responsible? The car owner? The car company? The research team that created the system? The state, which allowed these cars to move freely around their cities? A few brought up another problem: jobs were being taken away by this technology, the displacement of labour (the human driver), without a plan to mitigate against this loss. These people were largely ignored, and the issue did not come up in the political discourse as it was believed that it was the market's job to fix that problem.

After this media frenzy, the first commercial self-driving cars finally arrived onto the market. They could be driven in automated mode only in certain states, so the manual switch option was essential. They were faced with strong opposition by many groups: technophobes, political groups, lobbyists, competitors that did not have this technology yet, and parents worried for their children, because the news told them that these machines would kill their babies, without any conscience. Acceptance was not easy.

On the other hand, drivers who made use of this technology were extremely satisfied. At the beginning only people with special needs bought the cars (people with reduced mobility and/or vision, and the elderly), but then the popularity of the cars started to gain traction, costs fell, and word of the autonomous car spread all over. Traffic congestion, in states where they allowed these cars to drive, started to disappear, and eventually become a thing of the past.[93] Owners of the cybernetic cars were very happy about their investment and enjoyed the trips. They could relax, read the news, use their smartphone, do some work, or even just look out of the windows and enjoy the sky as if they were on a train. One could simply hop in, choose the destination on the GPS, and enjoy the ride. But the real 'killer-app' was the "bring me home" command. This was particularly useful in stressful or critical situations. After a long day of work, there was nothing that owners appreciated more than being able to go home without having to worry about anything. Even more importantly, they could go out with friends, get drunk, get into the car, and mumble "Go home", or press the big "Home-button" on the dashboard and fall asleep, while the car took care of the rest. Stories of how these cars were helping people and significantly improving the quality of their lives begin to get out: editorials in newspapers, interviews on TV, and a few celebrity endorsements . Traffic congestion continued to decrease, and the number of accidents started to fall significantly. The situation seemed to be changing, and public opinion became mostly favourable. Then, the first major accident happened.

A self-driving car was roaming around as usual, when another car, driven by a human, crashed into it. The person driving the old-fashioned vehicle was exceeding the speed limit and not following the street signs either. In short, it was his fault. The cybernetic car tried to avoid the collision, but the other car was simply travelling too fast and it all happened too quickly. The result: the driver of the old car, and his passenger, died. News stories went nuts. Headlines like "Self-driving car kills 2 people", "The killer-machine", and "Who 's going to pay for this?" dominated the news arena. The families of the victims were interviewed on national TV, and their pain and anger fermented the hatred towards the new machines that had been dormant up until then. "I knew this would happen" – "You can?t trust a machine" – "I voted against this law" – "We are going to do whatever necessary to ensure that this does not happen again", and other nonsense like this was spat out through every corner of the news. Only a few brought out the fact that, between the time self-driving cars and the first major accident happened, thousands of accidents among human drivers had occurred, with hundreds of fatalities, none of which had made it into the news. It didn?t seem to matter: facts are not important, what counted was people?s perception of reality. Some states declared that they would never allow these infernal machines to do any more damage, and refused to accept them. More legislation, more public discourse, more debates and opposition soon followed.

Meanwhile, technology advanced exponentially: the cars became even more reliable, they required less energy, their algorithms improved. They became cheaper and more widespread. More companies developed such technologies, and demand for these cars rose. Soon, it became the only growing market in the automobile industry, and companies that failed to innovate risked dying off. On the other hand, there remained a small group of dedicated individuals who continued to talk about the pleasure of driving, the value of keeping your mind occupied and the "good old days". They also claimed that it was important to have control over our tools, and that the direction people were taking was ugly and dangerous. The had a few supporters and remained faithful to this view in spite of the ever-growing advancements in the field.

After a few years, these cars became commonplace across most developed countries, there were still hybrid models, but people relied on their driving skills less and less. Roads became more safe, and the number of traffic jams was greatly reduced. Some bold companies began to design entirely new car concepts: fully autonomous, cybernetic vehicles, where the human driver is no longer needed. As such, they could redesign the cabin from the ground up. Seats could now move in any direction, all four people could face each other if they liked, in circle. Being in a car now became a whole different experience; it could be a truly social event. Given the situation, one would expect every car, bus, truck, and taxi to run autonomously by now. It would certainly have been the right choice: more efficient, less accidents, less traffic jams, cheaper and more reliable than human drivers... having only autonomous vehicles would be logical. But things do not always go according to what is logical. They follow complex dynamics that have to do with society, group thinking and complex dynamics that have little to do with technology and what is good; and a lot to do with politics, marketing, emotional attachments, old habit, delusions, beliefs, and what appears to be good.

The invention and creation of a technology may be a challenging problem, but sometimes social acceptance of that technology is a much harder one.

CHAPTER 8

SOCIAL ACCEPTANCE

Even though a technology might be tested, reliable, and ready for use, its social acceptance is not obvious at all. Fear, uncertainty, doubt, ignorance, and special interests all converge to stifle innovation and the betterment of our lives. Take what is arguably the greatest revolution in the history of humanity: the Internet. An ocean of possibilities: democratisation of information, distributed free sharing of ideas, instant communication across the globe, the levelling of race and class; anybody, anywhere, has the same opportunity. That was the potential. The reality? A handful of companies control the essential services for accessing the Internet, and an equally small number of private corporations make up a very large portion of Internet traffic. Even though we have the technology and the capability to provide the world's 7 billion people with free and unrestricted Internet access, only one third of the world is connected to the global mind.[94]

And even when the Internet manages to reach the people, things do not go exactly as expected. Politics should ensure freedom of speech, but attempts to censor the Internet are widespread, and increasing around the world. A quick look at the 2011 edition of Freedom House's report *Freedom on the Net* gives us a very depressing view. Of the 37 countries surveyed, 8 were rated as "free" (22%), 18 as "partly free" (49%), and 11 as "not free" (30%)[95]. The study's findings indicate that the threats to Internet freedom are growing and have become more diverse. Cyber attacks, politically motivated censorship, and government control over Internet infrastructure have emerged as especially prominent threats. And even among those few considered "free", there is a catch. For example, the United States of America is supposedly "free", but there is a long history of proposed federal and state laws that attempted to restrict access to certain websites and services, or to control people.[96] Some of these laws began with good intentions, but they were easily distorted and taken advantage of. The latest flavour of these obscenities was called SOPA (Stop Online Piracy Act), and together with its twin sister, the PROTECT IP Act (Preventing Real Online Threats to Economic Creativity and Theft of Intellectual Property Act of 2011; United States Senate Bill S.968), which gave the entertainment industry the power to censor the Internet. Videomaker Kirby Ferguson explained it quite nicely[97]:

> *"Protect-IP will not stop piracy but it will introduce vast potential for censorship and abuse, while making the web less safe and less reliable. This is the Internet we are talking about, it is a vital and vibrant medium and our government is tampering with its basic structure so people will maybe buy more Hollywood movies. But Hollywood movies do not get grassroots candidates elected, they do not overthrow corrupt regimes, and the entire entertainment industry doesn't even contribute that much to our economy. The Internet does all these and more. Corporations already have tools to fight piracy. They have the power to take down specific content, to sue peer-to-peer software companies out of existence, and to sue journalists just for talking about how to copy a DVD. They have a history of stretching and abusing their powers. They tried to take a baby video off YouTube just for the music playing in the background. They have used legal penalties written for large scale commercial piracy to go after families and children. They even sued to ban the VCR and first MP3 players. So the question is: How far will they take all this? The answer at this point is obvious: as far as we will let them."*

On January 18, 2012, the English Wikipedia, Reddit, and another 7,000 other smaller websites coordinated a service blackout, to raise awareness against this madness. That day, more than 160 million people viewed Wikipedia's banner; the Electronic Frontier Foundation, Google and many others collected several million signatures, many started to boycott companies that supported the legislation, and a rally was held in New York City with thousands of activists.[98] By pulling together our strengths and collective effort we were able to kill this monstrosity, but they are already coming back with other equally (if not more disturbing) idiotic proposals.[99]

Politicians are not only ignorant of how basic things work where technology is concerned, they also essentially act as representatives of corporations. To be more specific, their supposed ignorance allows them to have the paying lobbyists write the bills in the manner that most benefits our purported representatives? true constituency - the corporations and their owners, who are not satisfied with the majority of the pie, but want the whole thing. This is a problem with allowing money to act as a form of 'free speech'. It is an arms race with more and more money trying to buy the 'right' laws, and the people (corporations) who financially benefit from those laws, will always have more money to buy more laws.[100] This is not a cynical view, nor it is a conspiracy hypothesis. It is a well-documented fact that the top 0.1% of the US earns half of all capital gains.[101]

As if this were not enough, politicians and big corporations are only a very small part of the problem. Studies have shown that the public's ability to understand everyday problems and challenges is depressingly low. In the US about 87% of the people cannot even perform moderately complex tasks (such as reading and understanding a newspaper article about foreign affairs, comparing two viewpoints in an editorial, reading a graph, or comparing percentages) and 22% are functionally illiterate.[102] The same goes for Italy, the United Kingdom, Belgium, Australia, Canada, and many other developed countries.[103] It should come as no surprise if the public perception of complex issues is skewed. How can you expect at least 60% of the population to be informed and act responsibly if more than 60% of the people do not even know what 60% means? Consider the issue of climate change (which the popular press likes to call "global warming"). For years it has been at the centre of debate in newspapers and political talks. As if it was a matter of opinion. As if journalists, politicians, economists or any other person who was not a climatologist had anything meaningful to say on this topic. For years people have debated and discussed, and presented "evidence" in favour and against the "theory of anthropogenic global warming". In March 2010 a Gallup Poll revealed that 48% of Americans believed that *"the seriousness of global warming is generally exaggerated"*, up from 41% in 2009 and 30% in 2006.[104] Similar frightening results have been found in the UK and many other places.[105] We know that climate change is happening, we know that we are largely responsible for it,[106] and even the top climate sceptics admitted they were wrong to doubt global-warming data, confirmed by studies funded by the very people who denied climate change and wanted to disprove it.[107] Yet, a combination of bad news reporting, political trash-talk, pseudoscience, and public ignorance make it still very hard for science to go forward.

Fear, uncertainty, doubt, and ignorance are major obstacles to the widespread acceptance of life-ameliorating technologies, but they are not the only ones. Consider the automated checkout lines at the supermarket. If properly developed, using the right implementation with an intuitive interface, it would speed up the process, reduce inefficiencies and stress, but, of course, would displace millions of people.

Finally, there are other reasons why automation will not displace the totality of the workforce, even in those areas where it potentially could. Consider a restaurant. Some people think that a restaurant is a place where you eat, and that is what you pay for. Wrong. Such is the description of a fast-food line. In a restaurant, you pay for the *experience* of eating a good meal, you pay for the whole context, not just the meal itself. If they were to serve scrumptiously delicious food, but they had shit on the floor, you would most certainly ask for a refund, or walk away entirely. When you enter a restaurant, you expect to be given a pleasant context in which to enjoy your meal. The quiet atmosphere as you enter, the warm lights as you sit down at the table, the waiter who welcomes you and offers a suggestion on the wine to choose; all of these are elements that count in creating a compelling experience. Eliminating the human element from this picture may be harder than some technology enthusiasts like to think. People enjoy the company of other human beings, they like to empathise with them, hear and tell stories, exchange interests and different viewpoints. Even though the interaction you might have with a waiter is very limited, it can nonetheless be very compelling, and one of the reasons you decide to go to a high class restaurant instead of a fast food outlet. Picture now a holographic image of beautiful lady, who knows all of our interests, remembers when we came in last time, with whom, and ask questions accordingly, always with a gentle voice. This is an example often given by techno-geeks in favour of automation,[108] but I do not think that many people would be very happy with that – at least not for a while.

As you can see, the process of acceptance for any scientific evidence, disruptive technology, or anything that may change our way of living is not linear and predictable. Many obstacles are in the way, and opposition may come from all directions, for a variety of reasons.

With this in mind, let us analyse the whole workforce as it currently stands, and project into the future the possible consequences that accelerating technological change could bring.

CHAPTER 9

UNEMPLOYMENT TOMORROW

W e will analyse the US workforce layer by layer. I chose the US mainly for three reasons: 1) it represents one of the biggest economies on the planet, 2) it has very good public data available, and 3) many of the industrialised countries are in a very similar situation.

In the United States, as of 2010, there were about 139 million workers, with a population of 308 million.[109] The unemployment rate has fluctuated over time, but the cycles of ups and downs have started to look more like a trend. That trend represents a global rise in unemployment.

In 2010 unemployment was 9.6%,[110] one of the highest in US history, second only to the 1982 value of 9.7%.[111] An even more interesting statistic is the number of working people, against the total number of people. In 2000 the US had a population of 281,421,000, with a working force of 136,891,000. By 2010, the population had increased to 308,745,000, but the working force was only 139,064,000 (see Table 9.1).

Year	Total Population	Employed
2000	281,421,000	136,891,000 (48.6%)
2010	308,745,000	139,064,000 (45.0%)

Table 9.1: Total US workforce in between 2000 and 2010.

There are far more jobless people in the United States, and in the rest of the world, than you might think. While the reports say that unemployment in the past two years has been falling, the reality is different. As recent as March 2012, Eurozone unemployment hit the record high level 10.9%.[112] But there is more.

In 2011, in addition to the millions of unemployed, another 86 million Americans were not counted in the labour force, because they did not keep up a regular job search. Most of them were either under age 25 or over age 65.[113] It is

AMERICANS NOT IN THE LABOR FORCE, BY AGE

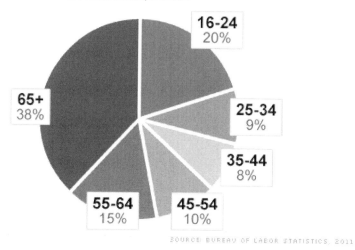

Figure 9.1: Americans not in the labour force, by age, as of 2011. Image courtesy of CNN, data comes from the US Bureau Labor of Statistics.

easy for politicians and economists to minimise the fear of unemployment, just change the way you measure and you are suddenly much better off!

This is the present situation, and it is not looking good. But what does the future have in store for us? Let us take a look at the number of jobs per occupation, with at least 1 million workers.

Occupation	Number of workers	Percentage of workers%
Driver/sales workers, bus and truck drivers	3,628,000	2.61%
Retail salespersons	3,286,000	2.36%
First-line supervisors/managers of retail sales workers	3,132,000	2.25%
Cashiers	3,109,000	2.24%
Secretaries and administrative assistants	3,082,000	2.22%
Managers, all other	2,898,000	2.08%
Sales representatives, wholesale, manufacturing, real estate, insurance, advertising	2,865,000	2.06%
Registered nurses	2,843,000	2.04%
Elementary and middle school teachers	2,813,000	2.02%
Janitors and building cleaners	2,186,000	1.57%
Waiters and waitresses	2,067,000	1.49%
Cooks	1,951,000	1.40%
Nursing, psychiatric, and home health aides	1,928,000	1.39%
Customer service representatives	1,896,000	1.36%
Laborers and freight, stock, and material movers, hand	1,700,000	1.22%
Accountants and auditors	1,646,000	1.18%
First-line supervisors/managers of office and administrative support workers	1,507,000	1.08%
Chief executives	1,505,000	1.08%
Stock clerks and order fillers	1,456,000	1.05%
Maids and housekeeping cleaners	1,407,000	1.01%
Postsecondary teachers	1,300,000	0.93%
Bookkeeping, accounting, and auditing clerks	1,297,000	0.93%
Receptionists and information clerks	1,281,000	0.92%
Construction laborers	1,267,000	0.91%
Child care workers	1,247,000	0.90%
Carpenters	1,242,000	0.89%
Secondary school teachers	1,221,000	0.88%

Grounds maintenance workers	1,195,000	0.86%
Financial managers	1,141,000	0.82%
First-line supervisors/managers of non-retail sales workers	1,131,000	0.81%
Construction managers	1,083,000	0.78%
Lawyers	1,040,000	0.75%
Computer software engineers	1,026,000	0.74%
General and operations managers	1,007,000	0.72%
Total of Occupations Listed Above	63,383,000	45.58%
All Other Occupations	75,681,000	54.42%
Total Employment	139,064,000	100.00%

Take a good look at the table above. Now answer this: how many occupations were created in the last 50 years? The 34 occupations listed above make up 45.58% of the US Workforce. How many new jobs were introduced because of the advances in technology? The answer is only one: computer and software engineers. This profession barely makes it into the list at all. In fact, if we were to exclude the bottom two, we would still have 44.12% of the economy represented, and not a single type job was created in the last 50 to 60 years.

The reality is that the new jobs created by technology employ a very small fraction of people, and even those jobs tend to disappear soon after they are created. Think of the jobs created in the IT industry in the 1980s, and how many of them survive to this day in 2012. If you were a programmer back then, or a system administrator, and you did not study and learn the latest developments, it would be very hard to find a job for you today. How many occupations were created because of the introduction of a new technology, only to disappear because an even newer technology came along? New jobs require a high level of education, flexibility, intelligence, entrepreneurship – most people have not been trained to be like that. In fact, our entire educational system was created just after the industrial revolution, with the idea of creating factory workers. The needed manual jobs, repetitive jobs, and our educational system has not been sufficiently upgraded since then.

The economy has been in need of a different breed of people for a long time. The process of changing that is very slow, and hard, however. One reason is because the teachers themselves have been taught to be the way they are by their generation of teachers. Standardised tests, standardised courses, standardises exams, can only result in standardised minds. Students are not encouraged to challenge the textbook, or the teacher. They are not encouraged to work in groups, to collaborate, or to find different solutions.[114] They have been taught that there is always a solution. There is only one, and it can be found within the book. But do not look, because that is cheating.[115]

The reality is that there are many solutions to an infinite number of problems. Some are better than others. Sometimes, there are no solutions at all. Sometimes the solution can only be found through interdisciplinary thinking, by collaborating with people from different areas of speciality.

There have been attempts to reform the educational system, and some great experiments are being performed (we shall explore this in more details in Part 3: Solutions). But the educational system is an even bigger and slower elephant than companies are, and it will take a long time before it adjusts itself. The question is, can it be quick enough to adapt at the same speed of technological advancement? I don?t think it can. A few people will be smart enough to adapt to this new paradigm (if you are reading this book it means you are already thinking about this problem, and you have a good chance of being in that tiny slot), but I fear the population at large will be in trouble.

Just to see what the trend is, let us examine some of the biggest and most successful companies, listed in chronological order. You can see the year they were founded, the number of employees in 2012, and the average revenue per employee.

Company	Employees	Revenue per employee
McDonald's (1940)	400,000	$60,000
Walmart (1962)	2,100,000	$200,000
Intel (1968)	100,000	$540,000
Microsoft (1975)	90,000	$767,000
Google (1998)	32,000	$1,170,000
Facebook (2004)	3,000	$1,423,000

Table 9.3: List of multi billion-dollar companies over time and their revenue per employee.

I think you get where this is going. Newly created multi-billion dollar companies do not have strings attached, such as old workers from previous generations, so they can focus on efficiency from the start. Big companies with more than 20 years of age are like old elephants, trying to move through a very crowded place. They are heavy, and slow. They have lots of "excess baggage"[116] (bear with me), which they would like to get rid of, but they cannot.

New companies do not have these problems. They are agile. They can hire the best, and only the best from the start. They encourage automation, rather than resist it. They deploy all possible strategies to increase productivity; that is, the revenue per employee. Look at Table 9.3 again. McDonald's was founded in 1940, and the revenue per employee is $60,000. As we move towards present times, we see a progressive decrease in the numbers of workers (except for Walmart, but we saw before how that is likely to change pretty soon), and an increase in the amount of wealth that each employee creates. The last and most striking values are represented by Facebook, with a mere 3,000 workers, where each one is creating more than $1.4 million of wealth for the company. One could dismiss Facebook as just vapourware, a fashion that will soon be phased out. But consider this. In today's economy, one of the most valuable assets is not represented in physical goods. It is information. Personal information about us, our habits, our wishes. Who our friends are, who we date, what we think. We have become the product. Facebook has the most extensive database of personal information ever created in history, approaching 1 billion users worldwide, and growing. Governments, companies, and intelligence services long for that information. In fact, there is a significant amount of speculation that Facebook may be selling our personal information to such institutions for profit,[117] even though Facebook has rejected such claims.[118] Regardless of the veracity of these accusations, it is without a doubt that Facebook has an intrinsic value much greater than its total revenue. A number that is already impressive on its own, considering how little time it took to reach $4.27 billion, with just 3,000 employees.

So if new industries only need highly educated, smart, and dynamic people; and old industries are replacing human workers in favour of automation; what will you do with the millions of those who have no formal education and do not have the means to even start learning sophisticated skills?

I noticed two types of reactions from economists when confronted with this very simple question. The first type is to not see the problem to begin with. Such economists do not believe that technology is displacing human labour, so they do not even begin the discussion. The second type of response is to claim that people who make such arguments should spend less time talking about what they do not know, and more time doing what they are good at instead. They say that people like Martin Ford or myself are simply ignorant of economics, and that if we were economists we would know better. That may be true. After all, we are not economists. And we might be wrong. But that is not an argument, it is circular thinking, a self-reinforcing tautology with no substance. If you think you have a better argument, and you stand by it, then please present it and enlighten us. I have asked this question to many economists, and I am still waiting for such an argument to be presented to me.

Their refusal to offer an explanation is probably based upon the fact that they feel that this is basic economic theory, things that I should have learned in academia, and that there is no point in wasting time explaining it. But whenever I hear this kind of response, I am reminded of what the great Albert Einstein said[119]:

"If you can't explain it simply, you don't understand it well enough."

With years of experience in spreading scientific education and debunking climate change deniers, creationists, and all sorts of nonsense, I can see how Einstein's quote could not be truer. If mainstream economists see me as I see proponents of "intelligent design", it should be pretty easy to refute what I say. In fact, it should be quick to dismiss my claims with a few simple examples. After a year of research and discussion, I am still waiting for them.

Marshall Brain, author of *Robotic Nation*, gave a talk about job displacement due to automation at the Singularity Summit 2008. At the end of his presentation, he was ridiculed by one of the other speakers: "Have you ever heard of this discipline called history? We've gone through the same crap 150 years ago, and none of what you say has happened!". This is the sort of easy criticism that uneducated people make very lightly: it did not happen in the past, why should it happen now?

First of all, there simply is no historical precedent for what we are about to experience. While it is true that we found ways to change occupation by inventing new jobs and new sectors altogether, there are two crucial aspects to consider.

One. There is a physical limit to what the human brain is capable of. Sure, our brains are very plastic[120] and with training can greatly improve over time. But just as our physical strength, however much we may train, has been greatly surpassed by that of machines, so will our mental faculties. Biological evolution is simply too slow compared to the speed of growth of artificial and machine intelligence. Eventually this might change, but only if we allow ourselves to be "enhanced" by machines by merging with them. But I do not want to get into that discussion, which would require a book of its own just for the technical aspects, let alone the ethical implications. Let?s stay focused and grounded: we *know* that the second technology-enabled species (intelligent machines) is coming, and unless we prepare ourselves, we are going to be in trouble.

Two. Have we ever considered the possibility that finding replacement jobs, no matter what they might be, could be the wrong choice to being with? I'm sure that *potentially* we can come up with millions of all sorts of useless jobs in the future. Just a glance at what we have accomplished in the last 50 years should be enough make that argument very credible indeed. We have long since decoupled the usefulness of a job with its purpose. Historically, the purpose of jobs has been to make what we need to live better: food, clothing, houses, roads, cars, et cetera. But as productivity increased exponentially, we could have easily got those things by working less. Please note that this is not an ideology, nor it is wishful thinking. It is mathematics. Suppose you require x amount of labour to produce y level of wealth. Then, after 50 years, you only need $1/10$ of x to produce the same y. It is a logical inference that you can work less to produce the same as before. Obviously the workload cannot be reduced at exactly the same proportion because advancing technologies also increased our expectations as standard of living rise. But the necessities of life have barely changed at all. We do not need 100 times the amount of food, water, and housing that we did 50 years ago. We could have easily reduced the work week. Instead, we work more than ever before, on average. This is pure madness: the purpose of technology was to free our time so that we could dedicated it to higher purposes. Instead, our jobs have become the purpose.

In the past, jobs have been outsourced to China, India, Vietnam, and other places where people compete for jobs that in the US and in Europe would be considered slavery. We are talking about jobs that pay $200 a month for a 12 hour per day, 6 to 7 days per week. And people there aspire to get these jobs. They have little to no insurance, benefits, vacation, no safety rules, no right to complain. Sure, if you work there and you do not like it you can always leave the job, but somebody else will gladly take your place. It should be clear that we cannot think to outcompete them with a race to the bottom, by bringing manufacturing jobs back here at lower prices. It simply is not going to happen, nor should it. The days when a high school education, a lot of good will, and hard work got you a decent middle-class lifestyle are long gone. Those jobs that have been outsourced are not coming back, period. And even those overseas jobs are now threatened by the rapid advances in automation and robotics. The more companies automate, because of the need to increase their productivity, the more jobs will be lost, forever.

More than ever, the future of work and innovation is unfamiliar territory. New and exciting fields are emerging every day. Synthetic biology, neurocomputation, 3D printing, contour crafting, molecular engineering, bioinformatics, life extension, robotics, quantum computing, artificial intelligence, machine learning, these new frontiers are rapidly evolving and are just the beginning of a new, amazing era of our species that will bring about the greatest transformation of all time. A transformation that will make the industrial revolution look like an event of minor importance. This new era will create new opportunities, new frontiers for research and innovation that we cannot even begin to comprehend now. I have no doubt about that.

The problem is this: will we be able to keep up with such rapid changes and educate the millions of workers with no formal education for these new types of jobs? I think the answer is a big and loud "NO!??.

There are millions of workers with a high school education at best, and sometimes not even that, who are over 40 years old and who only know how to do either manual labour or jobs easy to automate. Any new job that we can come up with will employ a fraction of those people, at best. And these jobs will require a highly receptive, flexible mind, with profound knowledge of highly sophisticated subjects related mostly to the fields of biology, chemistry, computer science, and engineering. It can take 5 to 10 years to educate a young mind in these fields, and we are talking about a mind that is not only willing to learn, but that is also enthusiastic about the learning experience. How many of the millions of middle-aged, unemployed people are willing to reinvent themselves and start anew? And how many of those is the educational system able to accommodate? At what price? Even assuming that most of them do find the intrinsic motivation, how many can afford the time and the money required to upgrade their knowledge and skills? Most countries can barely manage to educate their children, and even so in most cases with disastrous results. I find it hard to believe that the government will magically find a way to make university-level education free for all, including the millions of new students that will suddenly have to go back to school at 50 years of age.

The idea that society can keep up the number of jobs given the exponential expansion of technology, the rise of automation, and the widespread develop-ment of cheap personalised home manufacturing, is simply unrealistic. I have read several books, watched hundreds of debates and interviews on this subject, and I have not so far heard a single argument to support the idea that we can make this work, or how.

Technological marvels like Watson are now starting to make even the hard-core skeptics suspicious.

The old jobs are not coming back. The new jobs will be highly sophisticated, technically and creatively challenging jobs, and only a handful of them will be needed. The question is simple: what will the unskilled workers of today do? So far, nobody has been able to answer that question. The reason for this, I think, is because there is no answer. Not in this system, not in the way it is designed to work.

I think that if we want to solve this most challenging problem of our time, we will have to rethink our whole economic and social structure. Rethink our lives, our roles, our purposes, our priorities, and our motivations. It is time for a paradigm shift, one that will radically revolutionise our social system. In this universe, change is the only constant. Learn to love it, embrace it, and you will succeed. Fail to predict it, resist it, and you will be swept away by the torrent of change that is about to crush our civilisation as we know it.

At this point you might be wondering, won?t these highly sophisticated and technically challenging jobs be automated, eventually? Given what we have learned about exponential expansion of technologies, the logical answer would be: yes, most of them. Sure, we will create new fields of research, and new jobs will follow accordingly. But these new jobs will be even more difficult, and the percentage of population capable of doing them will be narrower and narrower every time, given that the ability for technology to self-innovate is greater and faster than our ability to keep up with it. So this is a dog chasing tail argument, the total number of jobs required by industry will be gradually reduced over time, and each time we will have to reinvent ourselves, finding new occupations for the newly displaced people by automation.

This becomes very tiring after some time. It is a game you cannot win. It is unfair, and there is no way out. One begins to wonder if this is the only way, or if there might be another solution. In the next part, we will explore many candidates in solving this problem of utmost importance. We do not know yet which will be the correct one. Maybe none, maybe it will be a combination of all of them. Nobody knows for sure.

What we do know is that we must strive to find the best solutions, using our reason and our imagination. We may not succeed, we may even fail miserably in the process. But we could also prevail, facing any obstacle with courage and strength, looking into the future, advancing and evolving, and I feel that we can only achieve that if we share a common goal.

To paraphrase Martin Luther King Jr. and Carl Sagan:

> "We are one planet, we must learn to live together as a family or perish alone as fools."

Part II

Work and Happiness

CHAPTER 10

WORK IDENTITY

Have you ever noticed how, when you ask someone "Hi, what's your name, what do you do?", they usually reply with something along the lines of "Hey, my name is Bob, I'm an accountant", or "I'm an electrical engineer", a teacher, a plumber, a sales manager, an insurance agent. Notice that you did not ask "What is your job?". You asked "What do you do?". People assume that is short for "What do you do for a living?," which is even more revealing. When we are asked who we are, what we do, we immediately identify that with our job, because that is precisely what we believe it means. What we do is who we are, and for the most part, what we do is work. What else could we do? After all, we live in a society that is based upon the exchange of labour for income, and income determines our quality of life.

Since I was a kid I have been working to pay for what I wanted. At the beginning, when I was very little, that meant no more than helping out in the house, cleaning the porch and the dishes. They were small things, but they counted. My parents infused in me a sense that things should not be taken for granted, and that while some things are provided for, if I wanted something extra I should take responsibility and *earn* it. This sentiment has accompanied me throughout my life, and to this day I still think my parents taught me a very important lesson: that I should value people's efforts, their work, and that if I want something I should roll up my sleeves and get to work. Not to complain, not to ask for it, but to earn it.

As I grew older I started doing more complex jobs, from polishing industrial materials to gardening; but I was also lucky enough to make use of my early passion for IT. So I would fix people's computers, then manage small companies' networks and build websites. I was 15.

By the time I turned 16, I was not really relying on my parent's financial support. I won a scholarship for the United World College of the Adriatic, and moved away from home. Since then, I have always lived by myself, which is quite strange for an Italian (most of them live with their parents well into their 30s). I now have a Bachelor of Science, I graduated at a NASA Study Program from Singularity University, I started a company, and I have many years of working experience, both in national and international companies. I remember when I was 22, my boss entrusted me with representing the company abroad. He simply told me one day "Hey Fede, I need you to speak about the new software. Here's the ticket, and here's the address. I'm leaving now, see you in London in a few days." The client was our biggest, as well one of the largest multinational corporations in the world, so I was kind of surprised that my boss placed so much trust in my abilities, especially since I was relatively young. At the time I was working as system administrator and IT manager. I then moved to another company and went on to create the Web and Media department, which lead to the creation of a team that effectively tripled the size of the company in a little over two years. This allowed for the transformation of a small video production business into a comprehensive web, media, and communication company, capable of competing in the international market with multi-million dollar businesses much bigger than itself.

The reason I am sharing this is not to try and impress you. Far from it. In fact, my resumé is quite unremarkable (I pale in comparison to many young entrepreneurs who have founded multi-billion dollar companies in their twenties). I simply wish to give you some perspective before I elaborate on the next points. I do not want you to think that these ideas come from someone who has never worked a day in his life and hence could not possibly appreciate the value of work.

10.1   WORK ETHIC, WORK UTILITY

I think that having a work ethic is very important. And it is precisely for this reason that I think work is becoming meaningless nowadays. "Work hard and you will be rewarded". That is what people say, and I generally agree. But something is missing from this picture. We value work, per se, and we think people should work. But, have we ever wondered about its *utility*? Ask yourself what is the value of the work you are doing? Does it help other people? Does it make you happier? Does it contribute to improving our society in terms of culture, health, efficiency, empathy, compassion, creativity, and liveability? If I work just for the sake of it, then I am no more than a mere instrument. A puppet. A robot that blindly follows orders.

Let me give you a practical example. I am a middle-age woman who works in an arms factory. I build cluster bombs. These bombs are not used to fight terrorists or to stop armies (whether such goals are legitimate or not is a matter for a separate discussion).

They are designed to horribly disfigure and mutilate anybody who is unfortunate enough to stumble upon them.[121] Many of the victims are innocent children, who at one moment are playing in a field with their friends, and the moment after that accidently detonating the bomb and having their leg blown off. I know that. But I am still doing my job. Am I doing a good job? Am I doing a useful job? Do you think that I am evil? What if I told you that I have two children and the youngest one is sick, but the government is not helping enough. I could not afford to pay for her medication, so I looked everywhere for a job, but all I could find were some part-time jobs, and I was not making nearly enough money to pay for the astronomical medical bills. So I decided to come here instead. It is a horrible job, I know. I hate this job, and I hate myself for what I am doing. But they pay well, and my children can live. I do not see any other choice. Do you still think I am evil?

I used an extreme case to illustrate the point, but there are countless examples that are more subtle, and yet much more insidious. Suppose I am a lawyer. I would like to work on cases of child abuse, workers rights, class actions against big industries that are polluting the environment and killing thousands – things that could help alleviate the pain and suffering of many people. But, working on these cases does not pay well, so I turn to working for multinational corporations. I become a patent troll, harassing small companies that try to democratise access to cheap medicines. Cases like this one are not the exception, they are the norm.

The idea that if you work hard and do your best you will eventually succeed is a compelling and romantic notion of the work ethic. Unfortunately, in most cases, it is no more than an illusion.

It used the be different and sometimes you can find inspiring exceptions. But these virtuous examples are becoming increasingly out of the ordinary. In my life, I have travelled to more than thirty countries. During my journeys, I would stop and meet people who live on the streets instead of passing by them. I talked to them, heard their stories, shared food, and sometimes even slept beside them, on the sidewalk, or in front of a train station. The homeless, the beggars, the thieves, the drunk, the criminals. They are all symptoms of a system that failed to give them a fair chance. The notion that these people just did not try hard enough is insulting, to say the least.

While I do not excuse or condone criminal activities or acts of violence, I think failing to recognise that people are driven to take drastic actions by the circumstances in which they live is intellectually dishonest, and also shows a complete lack of empathy. Let us assume for a moment the proposition that these people were slackers and thieves to begin with and that they deserve the situation they find themselves in. If that is the case, why is there such an uneven distribution across nations of slackers and criminals? And even within nations, why is there an unequal distribution across different regions, towns, and neighbourhoods? Why is it that every carefully conducted study shows a positive correlation between the lack of access to education and economic justice, and an increase in violent behaviour? Why is it that these negative symptoms can be seen most pronounced in poor countries, as well as in rich, but very unequal countries?

During my travels and my studies I was lucky enough to meet people from literally half the world (about a hundred countries). I was exposed to their cultures and I learned extensively from their stories. The film they show is pretty much the same as the one I described above. There might be slightly different cut-scenes and photography, but the screenplay is very similar.

I was at a café just recently, and I stumbled across a black man who was trying to sell me some cheap and useless stuff so that he could make enough money to get by. I got a pack of lighters (even though I do not smoke), offered him a coffee, and had a talk with him. Before sitting at the table he looked like an uneducated man, with no aspirations and no interests in making his life worth living. But as soon as we sat down and I treated him like a person – like an equal human being – something very interesting happened. He dropped the act. Suddenly the guy, who was having difficulties articulating a few words just seconds earlier, became a fluent speaker of three languages. He told me he came to Italy as an illegal immigrant from Nigeria, where he studied economics at university and graduated, but could not find any job in the country. Nigeria is widely known as one of the most corrupt states in the world,[122] where even janitors have to bribe officials in order to get a job. The integration process through legal means in Italy was close to impossible, and inaccessibly expensive. He came to the country after weeks of dangerous travel through Africa, only to reach the coast of the Mediterranean sea, embarking on a near-suicidal journey on an inflatable boat, during which half of the passengers died. Since then, he has been trying to find a job, with no success. Racism, and fear of the unknown are still rampant, even here in Europe. Eventually, he learned to earn enough for himself and his family back in Africa by begging for money on the streets and selling cheap goods that nobody needs. He tried working a proper job, but nobody wanted him because he did not have papers (and because most people here in Italy are racists). And there was no way for him to get papers unless he had a job. Now let me ask you this: What choice did he have exactly? And how does this relate to the idea of the "work ethic??? Stories like this one are far from being isolated cases. Rather, they are becoming increasingly the norm. Some have it worse than him and resort to organised crime. They are forced into this behaviour by the inadequacy of the economic systems, across borders, to take care of their citizens.

Even regular citizens, who just happened to be born in poor families, do not have it much better. Statistics also confirm this scenario: social mobility has been declining significantly over the past years in most countries, particularly in the industrialised world. The United Kingdom and the United States have, in fact, the lowest social mobility among the OECD countries, as confirmed by studies from the London School of Economics[123] and the Journal of Social Science and Medicine.[124] The poor will stay poor and the rich will stay rich, no matter how hard they try.

CHAPTER 11

THE PURSUIT OF HAPPINESS

It was the late 1600s when Richard Cumberland and John Locke were promoting the idea that the well-being of our fellow humans is essential to the "pursuit of our own happiness"[125] and that "the highest perfection of intellectual nature lies in a careful and constant pursuit of true and solid happiness."[126] It was such a strong idea that was integrated into the United States Declaration of Independence, and is considered by some as part of one of the most well-crafted, influential sentences in the history of the English language.[127] *Life, Liberty, and the Pursuit of Happiness* are listed among the unalienable rights of all people, and such ideas transcend American society. But rights are not rights if people don?t have the same opportunity to exercise them. In that case, they are no longer rights, they are privileges. And privileges can bought and sold, just like anything else. So, forget what I think, forget what you think, and let?s just look at the facts.

As we have seen, there is solid research showing that social and economic inequalities are structural. That means if you are born poor, you are likely to stay poor, even if you work your ass off 12 hours a day. Similarly, if you are born rich, you are likely to stay rich.

In view of these findings the exaltation of the exceptional cases of slumdogs who became millionaires, promoted by the media, can only be considered to be a sick and unfair con – a fairy tale for the gullible, a cruel game that reinforces the status quo, leaving the poor to battle against each other for scraps while the richest can enjoy the copious meal.

Sure, some people are still successful. If you are really smart, very good at direct marketing, and you build strong social connections, you might end up making a lot of money. But for every one that makes it, a thousand will fail. It is just the nature of the system.

Let us examine an example. Camden, New Jersey, is a small city of little more than 70 thousand people. It is, pro capita, the poorest city in the US. It is also the most dangerous. In 2008, Camden had the highest crime rate in the US with 2,333 violent crimes per 100,000 people while the national average was 455 per 100,000. The city's real unemployment is difficult to determine, but it is probably around 30 - 40%. 70% of high school kids drop out and only 13% of students manage to pass the state's proficiency exams in math. The coming years expect to see draconian budget cuts and layoffs of nearly half the police force. Reporter Chris Hedges writes:[128]

> "Camden is where those discarded as human refuse are dumped, along with the physical refuse of postindustrial America. A sprawling sewage treatment plant on forty acres of riverfront land processes 58 million gallons of wastewater a day for Camden County. The stench of sewage lingers in the streets. There is a huge trash-burning plant that releases noxious clouds, a prison, a massive cement plant and mountains of scrap metal feeding into a giant shredder. The city is scarred with several thousand decaying abandoned row houses; the skeletal remains of windowless brick factories and gutted gas stations; overgrown vacant lots filled with garbage and old tires; neglected, weed-filled cemeteries; and boarded-up store fronts. Corruption is rampant, with three mayors sent to prison in a little more than two decades. Five police officers, two of whom are out on bail and three of whom have pleaded guilty, have been charged with planting evidence, making false arrests and trading drugs for information from prostitutes."

How can the people of Camden possibly pursue their happiness? What liberty do they have? They have only three liberties: the liberty to become criminals, the liberty to be victims of criminals, and the liberty to leave town. Now, imagine a whole region like Camden, or even an entire nation. There is very little people can do when faced with such adversities, especially because they do not know any better and they don?t have a chance to receive a good education. So, they respond with what they know: various forms of tribalism (gangs, prostitution, drugs, petty crimes). Is it their fault? Hardly. They were conned, divested of their dignity, and robbed of their chance to pursue happiness. Their feeble, angry voices remain unheard; their hands soaked with the blood of lost opportunities.

Martin Luther King Jr. said: "It may well be that we will have to repent in this generation. Not merely for the vitriolic words and the violent actions of the bad people, but for the appalling silence and indifference of the good people who sit around and say, 'Wait on time"'.[129] A generation has passed and we are still sitting around. Our technology could allow us to bring about the greatest transformation in history, where all 7 billion people have the same opportunity to pursue their happiness, fairly. But we are sitting around, watching American Idol,[130] or killing each other at the mall on Black Friday to get stuff that we will throw away in a week.[131]

One of the problems is that we still believe in the myth that a willingness to work hard will be rewarded – which may have been true a century ago, when the economy was based on real goods and corporate powers and financial institutions were not running the game. But today, it is merely a veil of illusion, a one-line sound bite, a marketing tool to keep people believing the impossible, the unachievable. The reason for the persistence of this delusion is mainly because we do not want to believe otherwise. We refuse to accept the notion that we cannot make our situation better, and that is because we aspire to be like "them." We would like to be in "the club." In fact, that is the main value that we have been indoctrinated with since birth, almost everywhere, across borders, across cultures, across religions, across languages. The universal value that is inexorably rooted in our minds is to become successful. And by successful we mean, of course, well-placed in the financial and social arena. And if we become successful, it must be because we deserved it. The more we worked , the wealthier we became.

There is undoubtedly a group of people that belongs to this category – business geniuses, inventors, and innovators whom we hold in high esteem and wish to emulate. These are the brilliant minds that have brought about disruptive change, be it in design, technology, business, the arts, politics or society. But there is also another of group of people who did not earn their position, and it may be significantly larger than you would think.

If hard work meant that we could all be wealthy then we would have a plethora of millionaire African women. This is what author George Monbiot had to say:[132]

> "The claims that the ultra-rich 1% make for themselves – that they are possessed of unique intelligence or creativity or drive – are examples of the self-attribution fallacy. This means crediting yourself with outcomes for which you weren't responsible. Many of those who are rich today got there because they were able to capture certain jobs. This capture owes less to talent and intelligence than to a combination of the ruthless exploitation of others and accidents of birth, as such jobs are taken disproportionately by people born in certain places and into certain classes."

Psychologist and Nobel prize-winner for economics Daniel Kahneman discovered that the apparent success of the ultra-rich is just a cognitive illusion. He analysed the results achieved by 25 wealth advisers across eight years and found that *the consistency of their performance was zero.* "The results resembled what you would expect from a dice-rolling contest, not a game of skill." Those who received the biggest bonuses simply got lucky. These are not isolated results, as they have been widely replicated. They show that traders and fund managers throughout Wall Street receive their massive remuneration for doing no better than would a chimpanzee flipping a coin. When Kahneman tried to point this out, they blanked him. "The illusion of skill ... is deeply ingrained in their culture."[133]

But it does not end there. In a study published by the journal Psychology, Crime and Law, Belinda Board and Katarina Fritzon tested 39 senior managers and chief executives from leading British businesses. Broadmoor special hospital is a place where people with serious mental illness who have been convicted of serious crimes are incarcerated. Board and Fritzon tested both patients and bosses for certain indicators of psychopathy. The results were astonishing. *The bosses' scores either matched or exceeded those of the patients who had been diagnosed with psychopathic personality disorders.* It turns out that these psychopathic traits closely resemble the characteristics that companies look for – great skill in flattering and manipulating powerful people, egocentricity, a strong sense of entitlement, and a readiness to exploit others. Finally, and possibly the most revealing, is lack of empathy and conscience, which doesn?t hinder their careers, but instead may even help them climb the ladder of success.[134]

Paul Babiak and Robert Hare point out in their book *Snakes in Suits* that the old corporate bureaucracies have been replaced by flexible, ever-changing structures. Team players are deemed less valuable than competitive risk-takers and psychopathic traits are more likely to be selected and rewarded. Their conclusion appears quite dark and disheartening. *If you have psychopathic tendencies and are born to a poor family, you are likely to go to prison. If you have psychopathic tendencies and are born to a rich family, you are likely to go to business school.* This does not mean that all executives are psychopaths ? many of them are very decent people – but it seems clear that for the past few decades *the economy has been rewarding the wrong skills.*

The world has changed a lot in the past fifty years. We used to work to make what we needed to live better, but we no longer do that. We used to think about what we were doing, now we mostly follow orders, even if they make no sense. Today, most of the economy is a 'ghost economy' of financial transactions, profit-maximisation schemes and computer algorithms, with little regard to their consequences. We allowed power to be accrued in the hands of a very few to the point of insanity. Today, a small group of 147 mega transnational corporations form a giant bow-tie structure, an economic super-entity that controls 40% of the entire world.[135]

What have we become?

CHAPTER 12

THE SCORPION AND THE FROG

One day, a scorpion looked around at the mountain where he lived and decided that he wanted a change. So he set out on a journey through the forests and hills. He climbed over rocks and under vines and kept going until he reached a river.

The river was wide and swift, and the scorpion stopped to consider the situation. He could not see any way across. So he ran upriver and then checked downriver, all the while thinking that he might have to turn back.

Suddenly, he saw a frog sitting in the rushes by the bank of the stream on the other side of the river. He decided to ask the frog for help getting across the stream.

"Hellooo Mr. Frog!" called the scorpion across the water, "Would you be so kind as to give me a ride on your back across the river?"

"Well now, Mr. Scorpion! How do I know that if I try to help you, you won?t try to kill me?" asked the frog hesitantly.

"Because," the scorpion replied, "If I tried to kill you, then I would die too, for you see I cannot swim!"

Now this seemed to make sense to the frog. But he asked, "What about when I get close to the bank? You could still try to kill me and get back to the shore!"

"This is true," agreed the scorpion, "But then I would not be able to get to the other side of the river!"

"Alright then...how do I know you will not just wait until we get to the other side and *then* kill me?" said the frog.

"Ahh...," crooned the scorpion, "Because you see, once you have taken me to the other side of this river, I will be so grateful for your help, that it would hardly be fair to reward you with death, now would it?"

So the frog agreed to take the scorpion across the river. He swam over to the bank and settled himself near the mud to pick up his passenger. The scorpion crawled onto the frog's back, his sharp claws prickling into the frog's soft hide, and the frog slid into the river. The muddy water swirled around them, but the frog stayed near the surface so the scorpion would not drown. He kicked strongly through the first half of the stream, his flippers paddling wildly against the current.

Halfway across the river, the frog suddenly felt a sharp sting in his back and, out of the corner of his eye, saw the scorpion remove his stinger from the frog's back. A deadening numbness began to creep into his limbs.

"You fool!" croaked the frog, "Now we shall both die! Why on earth did you do that?"

The scorpion shrugged, and did a little jig on the drownings frog's back.

"I couldn?t help myself. It is my nature."

This is a story often told in psychology classes to explain how vital is to understand the immutable nature of something. There is no point intellectualising, making excuses, and developing competing analyses – sometimes something just is what it is. We need to recognise the intrinsic nature of capitalism. It is an unfettered force that puts the values of money, profit, and the ultimate objective of economic growth above life itself. There are too many real-life examples to ignore. Unless we take steps to moderate the present capitalist system, a few unlucky people will be left sitting on a vast pile of gold upon the smoking remains of our planet.[136]

I closed the previous chapter with the question: What have we become?The better question is: What have we allowed ourselves to be manipulated into becoming? The growth paradigm is based on the assumption that growth means better life, therefore people must adapt. Jobs. Consumption. Production. The cycle continues.

CHAPTER 13

GROWTH AND HAPPINESS

"Too much and for too long, we seemed to have surrendered personal excellence and community values in the mere accumulation of material things [...] The Gross National Product counts air pollution and cigarette advertising, and ambulances to clear our highways of carnage. It counts special locks for our doors and the jails for the people who break them. It counts the destruction of the redwood and the loss of our natural wonder in chaotic sprawl. It counts napalm and counts nuclear warheads and armoured cars for the police to fight the riots in our cities. It counts Whitman's rifle and Speck's knife, and the television programs which glorify violence in order to sell toys to our children.

Yet the Gross National Product does not allow for the health of our children, the quality of their education or the joy of their play. It does not include the beauty of our poetry or the strength of our marriages, the intelligence of our public debate or the integrity of our public officials. It measures neither our wit nor our courage, neither our wisdom nor our learning [...] it measures everything in short, except that which makes life worthwhile."

March 18, 1968, Robert Fitzgerald Kennedy, University of Kansas speech

Income determines our standard of living, almost by definition. But have you ever stopped for a second to start to think if the economic component is really the most important one in our lives? Very few people question that, it is almost a given, a definition. If you watch the news, read the major newspapers, and listen to the political debates, it would undoubtedly seem so. Politicians get elected depending on how effective their campaigns are in convincing people that their policies will bring more jobs, and hence more economic growth, which for some reason they associate with words like freedom and democracy. News follow accordingly.

This is what I feel, what I get from living in this society and receiving news from our information hubs. It certainly seems to be the case, but I do not like to just talk about what it seems. I like facts and solid data, claims that are supported by evidence. Luckily, the information revolution gives us the ability to look for ourselves in public data records in a matter of seconds – unfiltered and uncensored.

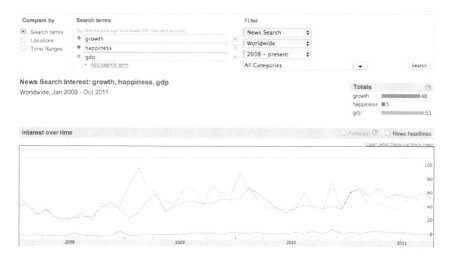

Figure 13.1: Google Insights comparison of the search terms 'economy', 'happiness' and 'GDP' between 2008 and 2011.

Figure 13.1 shows the relative popularity of search terms on the Web over time. On this specific search I compared the occurrences of the terms "growth, happiness, GDP," worldwide on news stories. Of course, this only applies to English speaking sites, mainly the United States, India, Singapore, Australia, the United Kingdom, and Canada. It is quite remarkable that the terms "growth" and "GDP," both economic concepts, have an occurrence about ten times as high as "happiness." You might object that "growth" applies to a variety of contexts, and that "economic growth" would be a more reliable term for comparison. While this is partly true (though unfair as it contain two words, thus filtering out lots of results), it does not explain why the acronym GDP (Gross Domestic Product) manages to outnumber both. Do we really think that *GDP is ten times more important than happiness in our lives?*

To be fair, how much we talk something does not correlate entirely with the importance we give to such a thing. But it does tell you quite a lot about the general cultural trend of a society over time, its *zeitgeist*. The news channels blare out many stories about economic growth as the panacea to solve most of people's problems. The equation that we have come to believe is that $growth = prosperity$, and prosperity, of course, is good. Not just that, growth is the cornerstone of virtually all economies of the world. We even use the word *recession* with a negative tone to describe the general slowdown in economic activity, including employment, investment spending, capacity utilisation, household incomes, business profits, and inflation; in which bankruptcies and the unemployment rate rise.

It looks clear enough what the *zeitgeist* of the news is. But what about literature, books, novels, and such? Surely they must differ – works by professional authors have little to share with petty news reports, right? In 2010, a group of researchers had the amazing idea to utilise all the available knowledge of mankind, and constructed a corpus of digitised texts containing about 4% of all books ever printed, or 5.2 million books. "Analysis of this corpus enables us to investigate cultural trends quantitatively. We survey the vast terrain of *'culturomics'*, focusing on linguistic and cultural phenomena that were reflected in the English language between 1800 and 2000. We show how this approach can provide insights about fields as diverse as lexicography, the evolution of grammar, collective memory, the adoption of technology, the pursuit of fame, censorship, and historical epidemiology. *Culturomics* extends the boundaries of rigorous quantitative inquiry to a wide array of new phenomena spanning the social sciences and the humanities".[137]

The Google Labs N-gram Viewer is the first of its kind, capable of precisely and rapidly quantifying cultural trends based on massive quantities of data. Using this tool, we can check how our culture has developed over time with regards to our areas of interest.

We can see in Figure 13.2 how "happiness" and "growth", between 1800 and 2008 have a negative correlation: as "growth" rises, "happiness" declines. Around 1830, authors started to talk more about growth than happiness. To be objective, correlation does not imply causation, and the mere fact of writing about something does not tell you the whole story. This data only shows the occurrences of such words in books, not their context, nor their meaning. Authors could well have been talking about the "loss of happiness", or something even more subtle. But it does show that the interest in "growth?? has been, well, growing, whereas writers cared less to talk about being happy.

Something very interesting happens in the last 50 years, let us zoom in and have a closer look.

Figure 13.3 shows how the correlation is even stronger. I took the specific term 'economic growth', to rule out other possible disturbances in context. 'Happiness' declines from 1950 to 1995, while 'economic growth' and 'GDP' rise. After

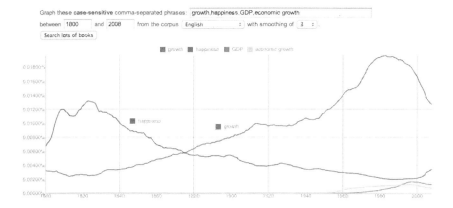

Figure 13.2: Comparing 'happiness' and 'growth' over time with n-grams. Courtesy of Google.

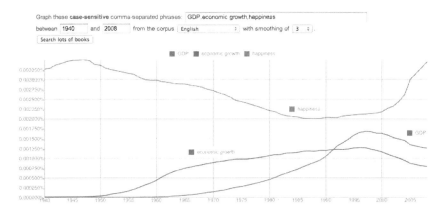

Figure 13.3: GDP, economic growth, and happiness from 1940 to 2008. Courtesy of Google.

that we observe the reverse effect: both 'GDP' and 'economic growth' fall, while happiness increases considerably. Again, correlation does not mean causation, but it surely is remarkable what this data shows.

For more than half a century, our culture has been fuelling the idea that the pursuit of growth, work, and economic expansion should be one of our primary goals in life, if not the highest of all. But that assumption is being challenged and it is slowly beginning to crumble. This very book that you are reading now did not come out of the blue. It is the result of the influence of this change in culture that we are experiencing, that has been increasing this past decade. As you can see from the graph, since the year 2000 there has been a steady change of course. In literature, there is now more talk about happiness, while interest in GDP and economic growth is eroding.

My initial motivation for writing this book was fuelled by the realisation that societies should move away from the GDP indicator and try to maximise happiness instead, using new measures such as the GNH (Gross National Happiness), the Happy Planet Index, or the Satisfaction with Life Index. That seemed to go well with the fact that technology was displacing workers more and more, and I thought a fresh look at the topic could give some insights into how to approach this challenge. Given what I have read and heard, there seemed to be overwhelming evidence, from sociological, anthropological, and other scientific studies, that monetary acquisition does not make one proportionally happier. That is to say, that there was no positive correlation between how much money you have and how happy you are. In a sentence, *that money does not buy you happiness.*

But as I checked my sources more thoroughly, I discovered that my initial assumption was not entirely correct. As a scientist, I had to look at the evidence and challenge my own beliefs, even if it was unsettling at first. What I found was a very complicated and intricate world of happiness research, which was much more complex than I originally thought it would be.

Richard Easterlin, economist and Professor of Economics at the University of Southern California, discussed the factors contributing to happiness in his 1974 seminal paper "Does Economic Growth Improve the Human Lot? Some Empirical Evidence."[138] He found that the average reported level of happiness does not vary much with national income per person, at least for countries with incomes sufficient to meet basic needs. Similarly, although income per person rose steadily in the United States between 1946 and 1970, average reported happiness showed no long-term trend and declined between 1960 and 1970. Basically, once a country gets out of poverty, there is no longer a strong correlation between income and happiness. This is now known as the Easterlin Paradox, which was later confirmed by a subsequent study, published in 2010 in the Proceedings of the National Academy of Sciences, reaffirming the paradox with data from a sample of 37 countries.[139] The paper concludes with the following remarks:

"Where does this leave us? If economic growth is not the main route to greater happiness, what is? A simple, but unhelpful answer, is that more research is needed. Possibly more useful are studies that point to the need to focus policy more directly on urgent personal

*concerns relating to such things as health and family life and to the
formation of material preferences, rather than on the mere escalation
of material goods."*

A possible explanation of the Easterlin paradox comes from a feature of cognitive behaviour that researchers call *adaptation*. If you improve your standard of living, you quickly adapt to it, it becomes the norm, and your expectations rise along with it. This leads to the so-called *hedonic treadmill*.

Imagine you are on a treadmill, and you wish to reach your ultimate goal – happiness, which sits just in front of you. As you begin to walk, so does the treadmill, at the same speed as you. In fact, you are causing the treadmill to move! You might be getting some small rewards along the way, but you forget about them soon after you receive them, because your real goal still sits there. So you speed up the pace, and start running. But the treadmill follows, and no matter how hard you try, you will only be chasing an unattainable dream, forever out of your reach. With more money comes greater and harder aspirations, which are increasingly difficult to achieve.

Another possibility is the *relativistic effect*, named colloquially "keeping up with the Joneses,", whereby we always compare our achievements with our neighbours. H.L. Mencken famously said "a wealthy man is one who earns $100 a year more than his wife's sister's husband."[140] It does not really matter how rich you are, you just have to be richer than those around you. Researchers even conducted studies asking people: What would you rather? Do you want to make seventy thousand dollars if everybody else in your office is making sixty-five thousand or seventy-five thousand dollars if everybody else is making eighty thousand? Does it matter how much money you bring home or does it matter how much money you make relative to other people? In the study people preferred to be making less if that meant making more than the people around them.[141]

According to urban legends, the opera star Maria Callas and the English Professor Stanley Fish had the same negotiating strategy. When Fish got hired into his department, he said, "I don't want to talk salary. I don't have a particular number in mind. I just want to get paid one hundred dollars more than whoever is the top person in this department." Now, there is a guy who knows about happiness (too bad it only works for one in the entire department).

In conclusion, as we quickly *adapt* to new situations, happiness is *relative*, and Easterlin proved that money does not necessarily make people happier. End of story, let?s move along.

Not so fast.

CHAPTER 14

INCOME AND HAPPINESS

Recent studies by Betsey Stevenson and Justin Wolfers, and by Angus Deaton, based on new data from the Gallup World Poll, find a consistent cross-country relationship between income and happiness,[142] which seems to suggest that money does make people happier.

But how can this be? The Easterlin paradox showed exactly the opposite, did it not? How could two scientifically valid studies that control for other variables, both coming from respectable and verifiable sources, arrive at diametrically opposite conclusions? This problem kindled an intense debate among academics, who have yet to come to a consensus.

As I was eagerly immersing myself in the study of happiness, I stumbled across the research of Carol Graham. In her two books, *Happiness around the World: the Paradox of Happy Peasants and Miserable Millionaires* (Oxford University Press, 2010) and *The Pursuit of Happiness: An Economy of Well-Being* (Brookings Institution Press, 2011), Graham provides a lucid analysis and valuable insights into the world of happiness studies. As she points out, it all depends of the question you are asking. Happiness is an umbrella term that describes a variety of feelings, not a single state of mind. In the Easterlin study people were asked an open ended question: "Generally speaking, how happy are you with your life?" – "Generally speaking, how satisfied are you with your life?" Instead, Gallup World Poll uses Cantril's "ladder of life" question: "Please imagine a ladder with steps from zero at the bottom to ten at the top. The top of the ladder represents the best possible life for you and the bottom of the ladder represents the worst possible life for you. On which step would you say you personally feel you stand at this time?" As you can see, these are very different questions – they create different contexts, and therefore mean different things. The first study measured Emotional Well-Being, which refers to the emotional quality of an individual's everyday experience – the frequency and intensity of experiences of joy, stress, sadness, anger, and affection that make one's life pleasant or unpleas-

93

ant. The second measured Life Evaluation (or Satisfaction), as in the thoughts that people have about their life when they think about it. Both studies could give different results, and yet both be right.There would be no conflict between the two results since they each measured a different type of happiness.

It seems we solved the paradox and things are finally clear. Except that they are not. Another aspect to consider is the *adaptation* phenomenon. As demonstrated in the previous chapter, as we raise our standard of living, our expectations rise as well. Analogous to the phenomena of adaptation to lower living standards is what Lora and Graham refer to as the *paradox of unhappy growth*. They observed that respondents in countries with higher growth rates were, on average, less happy than those in countries with lower growth rates, once average levels of pro capita GNP were accounted for. As it happens, economic growth often accompanies increases in instability and inequality, which we know makes people very unhappy.[143] Also, it appears that we are better at adapting to unpleasant certainty than we are to uncertainty itself. Graham continues:

> "While there are clearly stable patterns in the determinants of happiness worldwide, there is also a remarkable human capacity to adapt to both prosperity and adversity. Therefore people in Afghanistan are as happy as Latin Americans – happier than the world average – and Kenyans are as satisfied with their health care as Americans. Crime makes people unhappy, but the more of it there is, the less it matters to happiness; the same goes for corruption. Obese people are less unhappy when the people around them also are obese. Freedom and democracy make people happy, but the less common those conditions are, the less they matter to happiness. The bottom line is that people can adapt to tremendous adversity and retain their natural cheerfulness, while they can also have virtually everything – including good health – and be miserable."[144].

As you can see, things start to get very complicated.

While these studies looked at how the economic factors play a role in people's happiness between different countries, one could wonder what happens to people within the same country? Is there a correlation? Of which kind? And how significant is it?

Nobel laureate economist Daniel Kahneman and his colleague Angus Deaton at Princeton University recently published a paper in the Proceedings of the National Academy of Sciences[145] that addresses just that. They reported on their analysis of more than 450,000 responses to the Gallup-Healthways Well-Being Index, a daily survey of 1,000 US residents conducted by the Gallup Organisation. The study concluded that their life evaluations – that is, their considered evaluation of their life against a stated scale of one to ten – rose steadily with income. So the research shows that, within a country, income does correlate positively with Life Satisfaction. However, there is a catch. Life Satisfaction does not increase *proportionally* with income, but with its *logarithm.* Here's where the chapter on exponential growth gives us a big help again. Say you make $30,000 a year. An increase of $30,000 gives you a great bump in the rise of the ladder of Life Satisfaction. But as you climb up the ladder, you have to exponentially increase the amount of money you make in order to make a dent on your Life Satisfaction curve. Therefore, for a person making $100 million, another million or two will not matter that much, but a billion will.

On the other hand, their reported Quality of Emotional Daily Experiences (experiences of joy, affection, stress, sadness, or anger) levels off after a certain level. Income above $75,000 annually does not lead to more experiences of Emotional Happiness (or Well-being), nor to further relief of unhappiness or stress. Below this income level, respondents reported decreasing happiness and increasing sadness and stress, implying the pain of life's misfortunes, including disease, divorce, and being alone, is exacerbated by poverty.

In conclusion, it appears that money can buy you Life Satisfaction, but not Emotional Well-being. Lack of money can cause both dissatisfaction and unhappiness.

Where does this lead us? As we have started to see, this happiness business is getting more complicated than expected, so before jumping to conclusions there are a few things to understand about it.

CHAPTER 15

HAPPINESS

"Money can't buy you happiness. But it helps."[146]

*"I hope everybody could get rich and famous and will have everything
they ever dreamed of, so they will know that it is not the answer."*[147]

Happiness is a very mysterious thing. Its elusiveness is matched only by our desire to find it. For thousands of years, we have been looking for it. Some seem to have found it through deep meditation. Others by stripping themselves of all material possessions. Others have tried the exact opposite, accumulating billions upon billions of dollars, only to find themselves most rewarded by helping someone else, setting up non-profit organisations and educational or philanthropic foundations. Some find joy in simple, everyday moments. According to some philosophers and psychologists, humans are incapable of long term happiness by definition. For years social scientists, anthropologists, and economists have tried to determine what makes people happy. Up until recently, we had a lot of poetry and art about the subject, but very little data. We relied on common sense, philosophical insights, personal experiences, epiphanies; but we had no way of knowing if those opinions reflected reality.

The subjects of happiness, life satisfaction, well-being, 'the good life', and what the Greeks referred to as *eudaimonia* (a life of virtue and purpose), are all connected to each other, yet they are very different from one another.

So what do we *really* know about happiness? We do not know much, but we do know a few scientific facts that are consistent across cultures and nations.

First, we know that we are not biologically designed to maximise our happiness. We evolved living in small groups, we made strong bonds with even smaller circles of friends, we tried to pass on our genes, avoiding predators and fearing what was unknown. We might have been selected for seeking pleasure and instant gratification, but happiness is much more complicated than that, and it does not really come into place, evolutionary speaking.

Second, we know that part of what determines our happiness is genetics. We do not know the exact degree that it plays, but we know that it is there. A recent study by De Neve, et al[148] suggests that as much as one third of the variation of people's happiness could be heritable.[149] You might look at this finding and be disgusted at the thought of genetic determinism; or you might question its validity. Perhaps genetics does not account for one third of our happiness, but for much less, or much more. Frankly, I do not think it really matters (not at this point in time anyway, but maybe it will in 15 years.[150]) Look at it this way: the *majority* of your happiness *is not* genetically determined, that means there is a lot of room for improvement! Not to mention that genes are not the whole story. Their expression is what counts and some of them depend on epigenetic effects. Our biology might be responsible for a sort of "baseline happiness," what social scientists refer to as "set points,"; but external factors, our actions, and our reactions clearly play a major role.

Being happy, feeling happy, having happy memories, happy experiences, these are all different states of mind, and they cannot be represented by a single number. Understanding this fact is key in approaching the issue of happiness. Sometimes economists refer to Quality of Life, a loose term which defines the general well-being of people in their lives. That is, how happy you are. But not quite. Quality of Life is an indicator, a number, which does not tell much about you. It is a statistic, and a person is not a statistic.

Happiness is also very subjective. What makes you happy might not work for me, and possibly would not even work for you in a few years time. We are evolving organisms, our minds are continuously receiving inputs from the external environment and changing.

Such an unpredictable, mutable and subjective concept – happiness is serious business.

15.1   EXPERIENCE SIMULATIONS

Let us try a little experiment. Suppose I gave you two possible scenarios for your life. In the first you win the lottery, bringing home the whooping sum of $300 million. In the second scenario, you have a terrible accident and become paraplegic, paralysed from the neck down. The question is: which scenario do you think will make you happier, which will make you more miserable, compared to where you stand right now?

I am fairly confident that you would go for the lottery ticket. With that kind of money, you could start a new life, rejoice, and begin all sorts of wonderful adventures. Too bad that is not what happens. Chances are that after about one year, you will be as happy as you are today. No significant changes will be registered. In fact, most people who win the lottery actually become quite miserable, lose most of their friends, and see their family destroyed, along with their lives; whereas the paraplegic will come to accept his new condition, and learn to live with it. *Adaptation.* Even locked-in patients, who are completely paralysed, and can only move an eyelid at most (thus can still communicate), report levels of happiness about the same as everyone else. What is going on here? How is this possible?!

Dan Gilbert, Professor of Psychology at Harvard University, explains this phenomenon and much more in his international bestseller *Stumbling on Happiness* (Knopf, 2006). Gilbert notes that we tend to greatly overestimate the effect of major events in estimating our long term happiness. From field studies to laboratory studies, we see that winning or losing an election, gaining or losing a romantic partner, getting or not getting a promotion, passing or not passing a college test, have far less impact, less intensity, and much less duration than people expect them to have. In fact, a recent study showing how major life traumas affect people suggests that if it happened over three months ago, with only a few exceptions, it has no impact whatsoever on your happiness. That is because the prefrontal cortex, the region of the brain that simulates future events in our mind (among many other things), is a very bad experience simulator.

Psychologist Ed Diener found that the frequency of your positive experiences is a much better predictor of your happiness than is the intensity of your positive experiences[151]. Cultivating and experiencing many small happy moments is more effective and more rewarding than having a few sporadic big events.[152]

But how can it be that winning or losing an election, gaining or losing a romantic partner, getting or not getting a promotion, passing or not passing a college test, have far less impact, less intensity and much less duration than we expect? One reason is that we **synthesise happiness**. We think happiness is something to be found, but instead we *create* it.

This research is very well-known in psychology and it is called the 'free choice paradigm'. It is very simple. You bring in a few objects, say some Monet prints, and you ask a subject to rank them from the most to the least liked. Everybody can rank these Monet prints from the one they like the most, to the one they like the least. Now you give the subject a choice: "We happen to have some extra prints in the closet. We're going to give you one as your prize to take home. We happen to have number three and number four". This is a bit of a difficult choice, because neither one is preferred strongly to the other, but naturally, people tend to pick number three because they liked it a little better than number four.

Sometime later – it could be 15 minutes; it could be 15 days – the same stimuli are put before the subject, and the subject is asked to re-rank the stimuli. "Tell us how much you like them now." What happens? Note that this not in an isolated study, but the same result has been replicated over and over again, watch as happiness is synthesised. The subject consistently now ranks the print they chose higher than before, and the one they left out lower. Or, in plain English: "The one I got is really better than I thought! That other one I did not get sucks!". That is the synthesis of happiness.

To prove that this is not delusional thinking, lying, or an error in the study, they replicated the same experiment with a group of patients who had anterograde amnesia. These are hospitalised patients who have Korsakoff's syndrome, a polyneuritic psychosis that does not allow them to make new memories. They remember their childhood, but if you walk in and introduce yourself, and then leave the room, when you come back, they do not know who you are. They took the Monet prints to the hospital, and asked these patients to rank them from the one they liked the most to the one they liked the least, just like before. Then they gave them the choice between number three and number four. Like everybody else, they said, "Gee, thanks Doc! That's great! I could use a new print. I?ll take number three". The hospital staff member then explained that they would have number three mailed to them. They then gathered up the materials and went out of the room, waited half hour, and then went back into the room. "Hi, we're back." The patients say, "Ah, Doc, I'm sorry, I have got a memory problem; that?s why I am here! If I?ve met you before I don?t remember." "Really, Jim, you don?t remember? I was just here with the Monet prints?" "Sorry, Doc, I don?t have a clue." "No problem, Jim. All I want you to do is rank these for me from the one you liked the most to the one you liked the least."

What do they do? Well, first the ?Doc? checked to make sure they were really amnesiac. To do so they asked the amnesiac patients to tell them which one they owned. And what they found was that amnesiac patients just guessed. These are normal controls, where if I did this with you, all of you would know which print you chose. But if I do this with amnesiac patients, they do not have a clue. They cannot pick their print out of a lineup.

Normal control subjects synthesise happiness. What do Amnesiacs do? Exactly the same thing. "The one I own is better than I thought. The one I did not own, the one I left behind, is not as good as I thought." These people like better the one they own, but they do not even know that they own it. Think about this result. What these people did when they synthesised happiness is that they really, truly changed their affective, hedonic, aesthetic reactions to that poster. They are not just saying it because they own it, because they don?t know that they own it".[153]

As Professor Gilbert observes:

> *"We smirk because we believe that synthetic happiness is not of the same quality as what we might call natural happiness. [...] Natural happiness is what we get when we get what we wanted, and synthetic*

happiness is what we make when we do not get what we wanted. And in our society, we have a strong belief that synthetic happiness is of an inferior kind. Why do we have that belief? Well, it is very simple. What kind of economic engine would keep churning if we believed that not getting what we want could make us just as happy as getting it?"[154]

Indeed. The marketing tools used by corporations in order to sell more products rely on our inability to adequately predict what makes us happy. And so we continue to fuel the machine of conspicuous consumption – deluding ourselves that this will alleviate our sense of unease, and that instant gratification can create real happiness. We know that it does not work, and even so we keep making the same mistakes, over and over.

But there is hope. Becoming aware truly of this scam can help us escape the trap, and shift the direction of our lives, towards a more positive, genuine, and real state of well being – one that is based on empathy, collaboration, the thrill of discovery, and the drive to do something meaningful.

Chapter 16

WORK AND HAPPINESS

I feel like I am dwelling too much on this topic, but at the same time I realise that I have barely scratched the surface of the study of happiness. A more thorough analysis would require a series of books on its own, and even then we would only have an incomplete picture. In this book – as I mentioned before – I decided to focus the attention on the how happiness related to income, and more importantly to employment, since this is the main topic of discussion. As we have seen, research shows that there is a correlation between income and general well-being (albeit fairly complicated and multifaceted), but it is unclear if there is a *causation*, and if so, which way does it go? We know that happier people are generally richer than the average, but we also know that happy people are less stressed, more sociable, more productive, and therefore more successful. So what is causing what exactly? The problem of reverse causation and selection bias is a serious one. People who are generally lonely and unhappy tend to be dismissed when looking for a job, they are more likely to become unemployed and to *stay* unemployed.

Then there is another question. Would people be just as happy if they had the same income, but without having to work? Maybe it?s not work itself that matters, but what it represents: *Access*. Access to a good house, medical care, vacations with their families, movies with friends.... What if all those things were provided for, would they be just as happy?

The answer is a resounding... "NO!?? You didn?t expect that, did you? You thought I was going to say that if we gave people enough money or access to what they need they wouldn?t have to worry about petty little things and could finally concentrate on what really matters in their lives, which will make them happier. It turns out that just giving people money is not enough. We know that because people with full unemployment benefits were reportedly less happy than those who were employed, with otherwise similar characterises (controlling for other variables). Work does matter, after all.

Unemployment plays such a big role in our happiness that is hard to dismiss it with a few sentences. Many studies have found, in many countries and many time periods, that personally experiencing unemployment makes people *very unhappy*.[155] In their ground-breaking study of Britain, Clark and Oswald summarise their result as follows: "joblessness depressed well-being more than any other single characteristic, including important negative ones such as divorce and separation".[156] Great Scott! More then divorce and separation? Is being employed such a powerful force in determining our general well-being? Apparently, it is.

A while back we pondered about the possibility of reverse causation due to a selection bias in the income determination, could there be the same problem with employment? In other words, is unemployment causing unhappiness, or is it the other way round? Many studies with longitudinal data gathered before and after particular workers lost their jobs, suggest that there is evidence that unhappy people do indeed perform poorly on the labour market, but the main causation seems clearly to run from unemployment to unhappiness.[157] Other studies in social psychology also come to similar conclusions.[158]

Let?s stop for a moment and look at what we have discovered so far. Happiness is really complex, but we are beginning to understand it, and we certainly know more now than we did 20 years ago. We know that genetic, personal (stable partner, family, mental and physical health, good education) and social factors (democratic participation, sense of community) play a major role. We know that we are very bad at predicting our future happiness, as we tend to overestimate the effect that supposedly major events will have in the long term. We know that the memories of our experiences are distorted by our mind, and that we can be easily fooled. We know that we adapt to almost anything, with very few exceptions (noise, cosmetic surgery[159]). We know that it is hard to step off the hedonic treadmill. We know that happiness is relative, as we tend to compare ourselves with those around us. We know that income does matter for our life satisfaction (in a log scale), but only up to a certain level for our emotional happiness (about $75,000). Most importantly, we know that being employed is crucial to our general well-being.

If working is so important, and we are about to experience massive unemployment, then we are in for some very big problems. Unemployment leads to depression, anxiety, loss of self-esteem and of personal control. Numerous studies have established that unemployed people are in worse mental and physical health than employed people.[160] As if that was not enough, they also have a greater tendency to consume large quantities of alcohol, their personal relationships are more strained, they have a higher death rate, and are also more likely to commit suicide. Just to put things into perspective, a 1-percentage-point increase in State unemployment rates in the United States for 1972-1991 predicts an increase of suicides by 1.3%[161]. Now, try to picture what a 25 or 30% unemployment rate is going to produce. It doesn?t look pretty, does it?

At this point, it would appear that we have no way out. On one side we know that the profit-based market system requires an increase in productivity, which is achieved by automation. We have seen how that could play out – technology advances exponentially but our cultural adaptation does not. As a result, millions could be out of a job very soon, and only a few of them will be quick enough to learn new skills to find alternative employment. On the other side, we know that even if we find a way to provide for the unemployed, they will still live pretty miserable lives.

What should we do? Should we get creative and find them meaningless jobs, that serve the purpose of giving them the illusion of being helpful (even though they are really doing nothing productive)? Should we stop automation by enforcing laws to prevent the collapse of the system? Bear in mind that this solution would only work for jobs in the public sector, because corporations know no boundaries, and could not afford to operate at sub-optimal levels of efficiency for long in the global market. So should the states (most of which are broke already) somehow try to hire and pay millions of superfluous workers, in order to prevent widespread depression, suicides, and other collateral effects?

Before I continue with my wild and ridiculous mental projections, it may be wiser to ask ourselves "Why?". Why does unemployment have such disastrous consequences? Why do people have to work in order to be happy? What is so special about working?

Social norms greatly affect the subjective well-being of people, and this is particularly prominent among the unemployed.[162] If the social norm is to have a job, those who do not feel alienated and ashamed are constantly plagued by a feeling of inferiority. We know how significant that is, given that we tend to always compare our achievements to those of others.

Interestingly enough, this has also another unexpected consequence. The unemployed report to feel less miserable if they are surrounded by a majority of unemployed, as confirmed by many studies.[163] Somewhat paradoxically, a high level of unemployment will be very detrimental the people's well-being, but a significantly higher level would not be as bad. Before jumping to the conclusion that we should not worry too much about the future, consider the amount of pain and suffering that people will experience in-between phases. Also, what kind of society would that be? Remember that the reason unemployed people's happiness rises is because:

1. They adapt to their new situation, they lower their standards, their expectations, their dreams.

2. As it becomes the norm, the general culture of that society moves along with it, people lose purpose, and instead of being unhappy and miserable by themselves, they are slightly less unhappy and miserable together.

I don?t know about you, but I wouldn?t want to live in this kind of society. I shiver at the thought that this could represent the soon-to-be destiny of our species.

There has to be another way.

16.1   FLOW

"Choose a job you love and you will never have to work a day in your life."

– Confucius

The concept of flow was proposed by psychologist Mihály Csíkszentmihályi, and represents the mental state of operation in which a person in an activity is fully immersed in a feeling of energised focus, full involvement, and success in the process of the activity. It is a single-minded immersion and it is perhaps the ultimate in harnessing emotions in the service of performing and learning. In flow, the emotions are not just contained and channeled, but positive, energised, and aligned with the task at hand.[164]

"The 'me' disappears during flow, and the 'I' takes over. A rock climber in an early study of flow put it this way: 'You're so involved in what you're doing you aren't thinking about yourself as separate from the immediate activity. You're no longer a participant observer, only a participant. You're moving in harmony with something else you're part of'. Flow is a subjective state that people report when they are completely involved in something to the point of forgetting time, fatigue, and everything else but the activity itself. It?s what we feel when we read a well-crafted novel or play a good game of squash, or take part in a stimulating conversation. Mark Strand, former Poet Laureate of the United States, described this state while writing as follows:"[165]

> *You're right in the work, you lose your sense of time, you're completely enraptured, you're completely caught up in what you are doing... When you are working on something and you are working well, you have the feeling that there's no other way of saying what you're saying.*

Social norms, adaptation, income, and relative comparison do not fully explain why work makes us live more fulfilling lives. We know this because studies have shown that the self-employed are happier, even if they are working longer hours and/or making less money.[166] The same goes for voluntary workers, giving their hearts and minds to the non-profit world.[167] These people are not only working on something they enjoy doing, but also receive even more gratification through the act of helping others.

Another interesting observation comes from looking at the number of hours worked annually by a person against the average life evaluation.

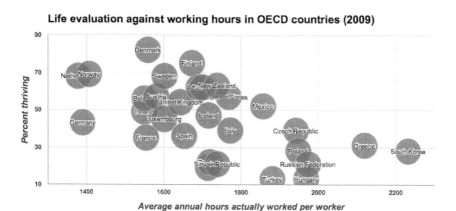

Figure 16.1: Life evaluation against working hours in OECD countries (2009). On the y-axis is percentage of people thriving, on the x-axis the average annual hours actually worked per worker. Happiness data comes from the Gallup World Poll 2005-2009 and working hours from the official OECD library. For a interactive version of the graph visit `http://robotswillstealyourjob.com`

Figure 16.2

As we can see from Figure 16.2,[168] [169] people who live in countries where they work less are consistently happier than those who work longer hours. Take Denmark as an example. It comes out on every poll as one of the happiest place on earth and as much as 82% of the population report to be 'thriving' (well-rested, respected, free of pain and intellectually engaged), yet they only work 1,559 hours annually, 200 hours less than the average of all OECD countries. Compare it now with South Korea, where people work 2,232 hours, 473 hours more than the average, and only 28% of them thrive. The same pattens can be observed all over: in countries where the workweek is shorter (Sweden, Finland, Norway, The Netherlands) people thrive; in countries with more working hours (Greece, Poland, Hungary, Russia, Turkey) people are more miserable.

There is an underlying principle at work that goes beyond societies? expectations, status and class, or the income they generate. Independence, self-determination, freedom, the ability to follow our dreams, the feeling of creating positive change, being in a state of constant *flow*. This is what *drives* us. This is the difference between living by the day with no particular thrills, and exploding with energy, living the days to their fullest, savouring every moment, making them exciting and indispensable. To make a difference, to transcend our condition, to help others, to create new things that nobody could ever dream of doing, to go where no one has gone before.

Drive, flow, purpose. Work is merely an *enabler* of these conditions, not a requirement.

CHAPTER 17

THE PURPOSE OF LIFE

If you live in the United States, Japan, and many countries in Europe, you probably heard your friends saying how busy their are. "So busy." *"Crazy busy!"* All the time. They can't even take a walk in the park without checking the calendar on their smartphone several times over, or spend unstructured, unplanned time with their kids. They are busy indeed. And they are also pretty stressed. But why is that?

I believe one reason is our socially-induced, compulsive urge to keep ourselves occupied, or rather to constantly "look busy". We start at a very young age, in school. Why do we have hour-long lectures when our attention span drops after twenty minutes?[170] Why don't we let children work at their own pace?

Then we continue in the workplace. Why do so many companies check on their employees as if they were babies? Why do they primarily pay based on hours of work, instead of performance? Why do we keep meaningless jobs alive, while desperately trying to create novel ways to keep people occupied?

I had many discussions regarding the issue of technological unemployment, particularly during my Graduate Study Program at Singularity University, NASA Ames Research Center, where I had the opportunity to speak with some of the greatest minds in the field, including the authors of the book "Race Against the Machine" Erik Brynjolfsson and Andrew McAfee, founding executive editor of Wired magazine Kevin Kelly, inventor and futurist Ray Kurzweil, and science fiction writer Vernor Vinge. I stand by my thesis, that the economy will not be capable of creating new jobs at the same pace with which technology destroys them. Many disagree with me, and we could have a discussion about that, but I think that is missing the point.

I can envision a plethora of futures where everyone has a job. One job could be to show up at the office, sit down, look busy, and read emails all day. Another could be to look at robots working, and make sure nothing is going wrong. The fact that only one in ten thousand robots fail over the course of a week, and that one supervisor per facility would suffice matters not. We can have hundreds of supervisors. And then supervisors of supervisors. And then managers, and managers of managers, at the top of the food chain. We can fabricate new diseases, and then create professions to cure those fictitious illnesses. Finally – desires, as economists teach us, are infinite, therefore we can perpetually generate things to fulfil those desires, however frivolous or whimsical they might be. While this may sound laughable to some of you, it may also sound striking similar to what we are already doing today.

After years spent pondering and contemplating on this matter, I came to this radical conclusion:

We must do away with the absolutely specious notion that everybody has to earn a living. It is a fact today that one in ten thousand of us can make a technological breakthrough capable of supporting all the rest. The youth of today are absolutely right in recognising this nonsense of earning a living. We keep inventing jobs because of this false idea that everybody has to be employed at some kind of drudgery because, according to Malthusian-Darwinian theory, they must justify their right to exist. So we have inspectors of inspectors and people making instruments for inspectors to inspect inspectors. The true business of people should be to go back to school and think about whatever it was they were thinking about before somebody came along and told them they had to earn a living.

I know, these words *are* radical. And possibly naive. The result of a young mind, oblivious to the intricate fabric of society, who has nice dreams, but no real understanding of complex systems and economic behaviour. As it turns out, that is almost a word-by-word quote of the great genius futurist Buckminster Fuller, interviewed in 1970 by New York Magazine.[171]

The point is that "We prefer to invent new jobs rather than trying harder and inventing a new system that wouldn't require everybody to have a job."[172] With this book, I have posited that robots will your job, but that's OK. I will go one step further. I would argue that *the purpose of life is to have robots steal your job*.

OK, let us be serious – that is not the purpose of life. But today, I think this is a necessary, yet not sufficient condition for finding your life's purpose.

I do not know my purpose of life, let alone your purpose, or that of everyone else on this planet. But I am pretty sure what the purpose of life *is not*. How many people have you heard, sitting on their death bed, saying: "Geez, I really wish I had spent more time checking that accounting spreadsheet for errors." Or: "Had I had a 2.5% return of investment on that deal instead of a pitiful 2%, my life would be whole". Nobody says that. They might be thinking "I wish I spent more time with my kids", "I wish I told my husband I loved him more", "I wish I confessed to my high school crush that I liked her", or "If only I had travelled more, I would have seen the world".

I was really moved by the story of a woman, who was a terminal cancer patient. She had two months to live, but her life's dream was to learn calculus. Then she discovered Khan Academy, and realised that she finally had that opportunity. And so she did – she spent the last two months of her life learning calculus. And she was happy.[173]

Another notorious slacker and good for nothing stated that: "The goal of the future is full unemployment, so we can play. That's why we have to destroy the present politico-economic system." This is no light statement, considering that it comes from legendary author and futurist Arthur C. Clarke (*2001: A Space Odyssey, Rendezvous with Rama*), who first conceived the idea of using geostationary satellites for telecommunication (we now refer to the geostationary orbit as the "Clarke Orbit" or the "Clarke Belt" in his honour).

But what does it mean 'to play'? It might be that Clarke was paraphrasing Confucius – "Choose a job you love and you will never have to work a day in your life". Or maybe he meant something different. Finding a job you love – one that is fulfilling and that allows to follow your moral code – is very hard today. In fact – according to Deloitte's Shift Index – as much as 80% of people hate their job.[174] We have to adjust our expectations to what the economy allows to do, and the sad reality is that many jobs are not fulfilling, and do not create value for society either. As if that was not enough, they are also going to be automated fairly soon – I suspect within our lifetime.

But – I am happy to tell you – there is light in the tunnel! The purpose of this book is not to convince you that automation will soon make you obsolete, but rather what to do about it. I have pondered, researched, and shared ideas and suggestions about this with hundreds of people; and I have compiled them in Part III of this book.

This is my gift to you – I hope it can be useful.

Part III

Solutions

CHAPTER 18

PRACTICAL ADVICE FOR EVERYONE

Finally, the time you have been waiting for. I apologise for having placed this section so late in the book, but I am sure you will understand the reason for doing so. Had I not explained the premises, many of these pieces of advice would not make sense, and then I would have had to explain the reason for each one – often resulting in overly long explanations, which would have diverted the attention from the main focus. But now you have all the tools, and the correct mindset to evaluate them critically, and they should make sense right away. In fact, you might have thought of some of them yourself as you were reading before, and this list will be a nice summary that organises your thoughts clearly and concisely.

18.1   NEED LESS, LIVE MORE

"The richest person is not the one who has the most, but the one who needs the least."

– Anonymous

The economy is evolving rapidly, automation is replacing human workers, more so every day. Unemployment is rising, and even those who still have a job are potentially in jeopardy. In a situation like this, very few are safe. So what choices do you have?

Self help books typically focus on how to maximise your income. Some of them are useful, more of them are hogwash. If you are lucky enough to pick from the good pile, and you dedicate a great deal of time and effort, you might be able to succeed (luck and serendipity also play a major role in the process). The advice offered mainly revolves around the following points: build a strong network of connections and high level friendships, be flexible and self-employed, and learn how to market yourself. That?s it! Typically you will read 400 pages on

how to do that, and then you try it out. While this might work for some people –
because *it does work* in certain cases – I see several problems with this approach
when talking to a larger public. First of all, it does not scale. The very nature of
the system does not allow everyone to be successful. It is a logical, as well as
mathematical, impossibility.

Suppose everyone became well connected, street smart, and learned how to
market themselves really well. What would happen? Since the system requires
you to have a competitive advantage over someone else in order to succeed,
those who want to excel will have become even more street smart, and develop
even more sophisticated marketing techniques. These people will then gravitate
towards each other, like more massive bodies in the universe attracting one
another, creating a new elitist network of even stronger connections. It is a
never-ending cycle, where the winners are always very few, by design. This is
not a bad thing per se, a meritocracy revolves around this very idea that if you
are better at doing something than someone else, you will excel in that area,
and your accomplishments will be recognised. I do not see a problem with
that, if you want to *take it to the next level*. The problem is that we are not
even at *the most basic level*. There are millions of people in highly developed
countries, and billions in the developing world, who do not have access to the
necessities required to live a healthy and decent life. Which brings us to the
other impossibility.

Should you dedicate your life to becoming more financially successful, thus
ensuring your ability to pursue your dreams? Or should you stop chasing the
unachievable dream of success, strip yourself of the material goods, and live a
life of austerity? Might there be a third way, one that takes the best of both? Is
it possible *for everyone* to live a happy life, while pursuing their dreams? It is
difficult to say.

The Greeks spoke of *virtue* (Latin: 'virtus', Greek: $\alpha\rho\epsilon\tau\eta$ – 'arete'), a sort of
moral excellence which valued as a foundation 'a principled and good moral
being', thereby promoting collective and individual greatness. In his work
Nicomachean Ethics, Aristotle defined a virtue as a balanced point between
a deficiency and an excess of a trait. The point of greatest virtue lies not in the
exact middle, but at a *golden mean*, sometimes closer to one extreme than the
other. For example, courage is the mean between cowardice and foolhardiness,
confidence the mean between self-deprecation and vanity, and generosity the
mean between miserliness and extravagance. To find the golden mean requires
common-sense, not necessarily high intelligence. In Aristotle's sense, virtue
is excellence at being human, a skill that helps a person survive, thrive, form
meaningful relationships, and find happiness. Learning virtue is usually difficult
at first, but becomes easier with practice over time until it becomes a habit.[175]

There is an idea, which takes inspiration from Aristotle's philosophy, that is slowly finding its way around think tanks, activist groups, and communities all around the world. The idea is that instead of trying to make more and more money or to abandon money altogether, we should try finding the golden mean by *reducing the need for money in the first place*.

This usually causes much misunderstanding, so let me be as clear as possible. Being rich is a relative concept. If you make $100,000 a year, but you have $120,000 of expenses, you are relatively poor. That is, you are poor relative to the amount of money to feel comfortable with what you need. If, on the other hand, you make $40,000 (most people[176] do[177]), but your expenses fluctuate around $30,000, you are indeed relatively rich. Reducing your need for money does not mean that you have to live a life of sacrifice, and give up the things you like. On the contrary. You do not have to constantly feel bad about what you doing. You do not have to take a u-turn and flip your life overnight. You can do the things you enjoy, and in some cases much more, with less. You can live a life of virtue, in the Greek sense, a life of greatness and fulfilment, without having to earn hundreds of thousands of dollars, and without giving yourself over to a life of austerity.

Some people refer to this as *downshifting*, and the idea is pretty straightforward. Live simpler lives, escape from the rat race of obsessive materialism and reduce the stress, overtime, and psychological expense that typically go along with it. It is possible to find an improved balance between leisure and work, focusing life goals on personal fulfilment and relationship building instead of the all-consuming pursuit of economic success. There is no need for dramatic or sudden changes that may jeopardise your stability, you can start with simple things, make a plan, build upon that, and see yourself living a better, more fulfilling, and happier life.

It sounds like an impossible win-win scenario, so what is the catch? The catch is that there is no silver bullet. No formula that will work for everyone. And most importantly, nobody that will give you a precise list of instructions that you just have to follow.

Not all of us can be physicists, biologists, computer scientists, biotechnologists. *You* have to find out what your strengths are, what you love to do, and how that can sustain you. We cannot all be mathematical geniuses or musical prodigies, but we can all find something that we are good at and that we enjoy doing. To achieve a life of virtue, full of passion and interest, while ensuring that you have enough to go by, you have to be smart and take a look at all the possibilities that come before you. And to do that you start by studying and learning new things, and expanding your horizons.

18.2   EDUCATE YOURSELF

> *"Give a man a fish and you feed him for a day. Teach a man to fish and you feed him for a lifetime."*
>
> – Chinese Proverb[178]

This old Chinese proverb has been true for thousands of years. But given the recent massive decline in fish stocks,[179] I think it needs some adjustments. So here is my updated version:

> *"Give a man a fish and you feed him for a day. Teach a man to fish and you feed him for a little more. Teach him how to be problem solver, and he can face any challenge that lies ahead of him."*

Whatever list of things to do I can come up with, it will never solve *your* life's problems by itself. It can be a good starting point, an inspiration, but situations are constantly changing, evolving, and *the only way to keep pace with the world is to educate yourself to be a critical thinker and a problem solver.*

Education has always been of great interest to me. I remember very vividly when I was at school, starting from primary, all the way to high school. It was one of the most painful periods of my life. I remember the utter boredom of sitting at my desk, listening to uninspiring lessons, learning series of rules, memorising numbers and words, looking at the clock, waiting for the pain to end, when it finally turned 16:30 and I could go home. But it was not always like that.

My mother is a librarian. When I was in kindergarten, she used to take me to the public library where she worked, until she finished her shift. There I was, sitting at the desk, with nobody around to tell me what to do, or how I should do it. I had the chance to pick up books of all sorts, well before I was able to read. My mom told me that, from a very early age, I was fascinated by science books. I was looking at drawings of atoms and electromagnetic fields, pictures of all species of animals, stars and galaxies, mechanical devices, dinosaurs, and all sorts of other interesting things. I do not remember much, but she said that, as far back as she can remember, I wanted to know about the world and explore all branches of knowledge. My enthusiasm and fascination for our universe were insatiable. Then, the time came for me to go to school, and I was hit in the face, like a bus at full speed crushing into a brick wall. I could not understand why the teachers could not – or more probably did not want to – answer my questions. But most of all, I could not believe that they were not even interested in what they were teaching! I tried, and tried, and tried, and... nothing. Disappointment preceded surrender.

I was considered a strange kid. I was always wondering about what the biggest animal was, how did we know there were dinosaurs 60 million years ago, and not 2 million, or 10 million (this was well before the film Jurassic Park come out), why were elephants so big, why did spiders have eight legs instead of six, how could the hummingbird fly and how fast did it flap its wings, why and how did planets form? To my teachers, these were irrelevant questions. I did not have to know the answer to them in order to pass the tests. They were not in the curricula. So why did I bother so much wanting to know more?

The frustration reached the point where I just gave up on the school system, and continued researching on my own. I did not leave school, though. I did as I was told to do and mostly shut up during the lessons, as required. But I diverted all my efforts in researching and studying on my own things that were outside the state requirements. I devoured every edition of the Guinness book of records and The World Factbook. I simply could not stop. It felt as if I were being attracted to the data, as if an invisible force was pushing me towards it. It was only later in life that I realised how to make sense of this information, how to challenge and verify its authenticity, how to contextualise it. It was not something that anybody taught me, I had to learn it the hard way.

Now, this was before the Internet became a widespread phenomenon. When I think of the immense effort that I had to put in in order to know and understand just a little more, and I compare it to how easy it is today, it simply blows my mind! What required dozens of hours of painful research, often through non-interactive and quite unattractive books, is now available in seconds, often in videos, lectures, and conferences held by the most amazing thinkers of our time. A poor kid in Uganda has access to more knowledge than the president of the United States did 30 years ago. Such a dramatic change has no precedent in human history. The invention of the printing press is a pallid, almost insignificant event in comparison. Today, it is possible to receive a world-class education, where the best teachers, coming from the most prestigious universities in the world, teach any subject, for free. This is such a mind blowing and revolutionary thought that I am surprised so few people are aware of it.

iTunes is installed on more than 400 million computers worldwide,[180] yet when I talk to people about it, very few know that it can be used for something other than music and films. On May 30, 2007, Apple announced the launch of iTunesU, which delivers university lectures from the major universities around the world, for free. These are high quality video lectures, often the same that you would get from a $200,000 degree, only that you can watch them at home, or on the bus, pause them, re-view them, and they do not cost anything. The materials are collected from a variety of locations around the world, including colleges, universities, museums, libraries, and other cultural institutions of educational value. There are currently more than 100,000 files available for download, from Oxford, Yale, Harvard, Stanford, Cambridge... There are literally hundreds of them. This approach was pioneered by OpenCourseWare, a cultural movement that started in 1999 in Germany, and took off when the Massachusetts Institute of Technology launched its MIT OpenCourseWare in October 2002. Since then it has been reinforced by the launch of similar projects at Yale, Michigan University, and the University of California, Berkeley. Similar institutes in Japan and China developed, and it quickly spread all over the planet. MIT's reasoning behind OCW was to 'enhance human learning worldwide by the availability of a web of knowledge'.[181]

This immense potential offered by this remains largely untapped in my opinion, even though things are quickly changing. The reason for this is the lack of personal motivation to follow the courses on the part of potential learners, as well as the difficulty of the material.

Now a new player has come in, and it has already started to change the game. It was the late 2004, when Salman Khan was discussing with his little cousin Nadia about the nature of the universe and other things like that. Nadia struck him as a highly intelligent young girl, who was ready to begin a career in the sciences in the near future. When he said that to her parents, they were startled, because the girl has been struggling with some basic math at school. Sal could not believe what he just heard. How could someone who was tackling highly sophisticated issues struggle with basic math? Something was wrong with the school system. He began tutoring her over the Internet, and that proved to be very effective. When other relatives and friends sought his tutelage, he decided it would be more practical and beneficial to distribute the tutorials on YouTube. It was November 16, 2006. At the time he was a Hedge Fund analyst, making quite a lot of money, and in the process of becoming a very successful businessman.

Money, power, stability. What more could anyone ask for?

Purpose. Sal was still working at his job during the day, while recording micro-lectures for his relatives at night. Suddenly other people began to watch them. More and more. And they started writing to him as well. One day he received this letter:

"Mr. Khan,

No teacher has ever done me any good – this may sound harsh but I mean it quite literally. I was force fed medication to keep me from talking and chastised for not speaking out when called on. Where I am from blacks are not welcomed with open arms into schools – my mother and her sisters had to go to a small shack two hours from home when they went to school. About five years ago my family collected enough money to move from where i was born, so that I could have a chance at having an education and living a real life. But without a real mastery of elementary math I was slow to progress.

I am now in college and learning more than I ever have in my life. But an inadequate math background has been holding me back. I found the Kahn Academy in June of 2009, right after I completed Math 141 (a college algebra course). I have spent the entire summer on your youtube page. And I just wanted to thank you for everything you are doing. You are a Godsend. Last week I tested for a math placement exam and I am now in Honors Math 200. No question was answered incorrectly. My placement test holder was so impressed by the breadth of my knowledge of math that he said I should be in Linear algebra.

Mr. Khan, I can say without any doubt that you have changed my life and the lives of everyone in my family".

A few days after that, Sal quit his job to work on the 'Khan Academy' full-time (http://khanacademy.org). The conscience and the realisation that you are helping other people, building an "emphatic civilisation",[182] based on the sharing of scientific knowledge, for the betterment of humankind; that is something worth waking up for in the morning. "With so little effort on my own part, I can empower an unlimited amount of people for all time. I can't imagine a better use of my time." – said Sal. The mission of the academy is nothing less than to "provide a high quality education to anyone, anywhere".

I bet you remember those times back in college, when you and your friends tried to figure out the intuition behind a concept, or how to solve a specific problem. It would take hours, a bunch of minds working non-stop to find a solution, and a considerable number of headaches, when finally somebody screams 'Eureka!' (or 'Fuck yeah!', in many cases). The person then explains the solution to the riddle to everyone else, which typically takes no more than 10 minutes. Would it not be great if you could just skip the four hours and have the teacher explain it in an intuitive and practical manner in minutes? I thought it was a mere dream, until I saw Sal's videos.

The whole story is absurd and fascinating at the same time. One guy who takes on MIT, Stanford, and Harvard, becoming more popular and appreciated than those established institutions throughout the world? One person who wants to build the biggest online school, centre for reason, art and science, by himself? Yep, apparently he is really doing it!

It?s been a couple of years since I decided I wanted to learn chemistry. When I discovered MIT OpenCourseWare and iTunesU I was blown away. Lessons from Stanford, Harvard and MIT recorded, available for free on the internet? Wow. "I need to take some time off to learn a ton of subjects", I thought. But of course, that time never came. I got back from work at 8pm, feeling exhausted, and while I enjoyed keeping my brain working, I usually watched a TED talk or a conference from the Singularity University, but it was too difficult to try to follow a course on Quantum Entanglement or Biochemistry at 11pm. With Sal's videos, in their 13-minute format, I could enjoy learning at any time of the day –at a lunch break, on the train, after dinner, you name it.

The concepts are easy, very well presented, and I cannot stress this enough, they are intuitive. I have always been interested in why something happens, how does it work, what makes it work, what are the conditions under which it does not, and so on. Anybody can apply a formula, especially computers. But can you derive the formula? Can you explain how they came up with it? With the advent of Wolfram Alpha,[183] it becomes clear that doing mechanical calculations by hand is pretty much obsolete nowadays. What matters most is the idea, the concept, the intuition.

I immediately started to follow the chemistry lessons from Khan Academy, and I felt the excitement of discovery and understanding every time I watched one of those videos. It all seems quite strange, but it makes a whole lot of sense if you contextualise it. The exponential growth of information technology and the advent of the free software movement has lead to a groundbreaking shift in our mental paradigm. Information is ever more accessible, reliable, and most of all free to all. GNU, Linux, Creative Commons, Wikipedia, OpenCourseWare, and now the Khan academy. It is a logical consequence of the exponential growth of technology and culture.

Sal expressed his desire to teach as many subjects as possible. As of now (mid 2012), there are more then 3,200 lectures, spanning mathematics, history, health-care and medicine, finance, physics, chemistry, biology, astronomy, economics, cosmology, organic chemistry, American civics, art history, microeconomics, and computer science. And it is basically just him teaching (although it is expanding rapidly with new great teachers). Surely the question must have crossed your mind: 'Who is this guy? What qualifies him to teach such a variety of subjects?'. Sal was valedictorian of his high school class and attained a perfect score in the math portion of his SATs. He has a Bachelor of Science in mathematics, another Bachelor in electrical engineering and computer science, and a Master of Science in electrical engineering and computer science from the Massachusetts Institute of Technology. As if that was not enough, he also holds a Master of Business Administration from the Harvard Business School. And he did all that before turning 32. He knows what he is talking about.

I wrote about the Khan Academy back in 2009, when (almost) nobody knew of it. Now, it?s the biggest school in the history of humanity. It has already delivered 150 million lectures to millions of students worldwide. And it?s just warming up. It received millions of dollars in donations from The Bill and Melinda Gates Foundation, Google, and the O'Sullivan Foundation. It was featured on CNN, PBS, CBS, TED, and Charlie Rose, just to name a few. It is expanding and improving every day. It?s being translated in more than 40 languages, and they expect to completely cover the 10 most spoken languages in just a few years. There are some schools running trials to see if this approach can be integrated in the classical learning environment. The preliminary results are astounding. Rather than rendering the teachers obsolete, it actually helps them become better mentors, leaving more time to do one-to-one, real-life interaction with students. Students can learn on their own, at home, and then have more productive time in school, by doing exercises together, solidifying their knowledge, or by teaching each other what they just learned. In Sal's words:

"This could be the DNA for a physical school where students spend 20% of their day watching videos and doing self-paced exercises and the rest of the day building robots or painting pictures or composing music or whatever."[184]

So the teacher becomes more of a mentor, a guide, rather than an authority figure. They have a dashboard of all of their students, they can see what they are working on, how well they are doing, and intervene only when students are struggling on a specific topic.

Sounds incredible? Amazing?! Too good to be true? So what?s the catch? It seems unbelievable, but there is no catch. Khan Academy is free. The lessons are in Creative Commons. The code for the website and the platform is completely Open Source. You can learn at your own pace. You can choose to follow only the subjects you like, or you can follow the suggested path. You can even ask your school to integrate it. Or you can use it on you own, then go to school and kick ass anyway. The lessons are fun, easy, and very intuitive. They are expanding rapidly, and improving every day.

What is missing from this picture? Two things: the lack of academic achievements, and the difficulty of teaching the arts and humanities through this medium. But I see none of them as an obstacle. As we have seen, things are evolving rapidly. Anything that is touched by exponentially expanding technologies follows the curve of accelerating change.[185] The educational system will have to adjust itself to realities like the Khan Academy, not the other way around. The reason parents send their children to school is not to learn (sadly), but to earn a degree, which will make it easier for them to find a job. And this equation is no longer true. As Dale J. Stephens, Michael Ellsberg, and many others have pointed out, traditional education is overrated, and what makes you competitive in the workforce is not necessarily your academic achievements. Sure, having a Ph.D. from Stanford helps, but it is not a sufficient requirement for success anymore. If your goal is to go and work at Google, PayPal, Microsoft, or any other of those technology giants, then soon achieving proficiency on the Khan Academy may look more palatable than a degree from a traditional institution. Smart universities understand this, and they are reforming pretty quickly. MIT just launched MITx, which offers a portfolio of MIT courses for free to a virtual community of learners around the world. It will also enhance the educational experience of its on-campus students, offering them online tools that supplement and enrich their classroom and laboratory experiences. With a small fee, people who follow the online course can also receive a valid certificate from MIT.

Last autumn, I took part in one of the first experiments of massive online learning, when Sebastian Thrun, Peter Norving, and Andrew Ng launched the Stanford courses on Artificial Intelligence and Machine Learning. They were still rough experiments, with ups and downs, but the results were incredible nonetheless. Hundreds of thousand of people participated in these 10-week courses, which were more or less like the ones that regular Stanford students followed. In the end, if you were good and did your homework right (all through automated software), in addition to having acquired a solid knowledge and understanding of a sophisticated and useful subject, you also received a statement of accomplishment, that you can put in your curriculum. The nice thing is that you followed the course week by week, and you had a class of thousands of people to work with, ask questions, and discuss the lessons and exercises with. It was a wonderful experience. Sebastian Thrun was so excited that he decided to leave his Professorship at Stanford and dedicate his time to teach to millions of students worldwide, for free (`http://udacity.com`). Sounds familiar?

The approach by Andrew Ng inspired many others, who are now teaching under the umbrella of a non-profit called 'Coursera', with high level subjects such as Model Thinking, Natural Language Processing, Game Theory, Probabilistic Graphical Models, Cryptography, Design and Analysis of Algorithms, Software as a Service, Computer Vision, Computer Science, Machine Learning, Human-Computer Interaction, Making Green Buildings, Information Theory, Anatomy, and Computer Security. Needless to say, this is just the beginning. It is the natural evolution of education when combined with technology. Embrace change, or die.

So, how does this apply to you? How does this help you? In case you haven?t noticed, this is your winning ticket. You can become an expert, or at least have access to the tools that will allow you to become an expert, at almost anything, **for free**. Soon there will be high quality courses on molecular engineering, nanotechnology, sustainable technologies for the production of energy, food, houses, anything really. Education will be ever more relevant, easy, engaging, and most of all, free. Today, the best investment you can make is in yourself.

The tools of creativity are in everybody's hands, and they are becoming increasingly easier and more accessible. You have an opportunity that nobody else has ever had in human history.

Carpe diem.

18.3 EDUCATE OTHERS

Now, what good is saving yourself, if everyone else fails? Don?t keep this knowledge to yourself, share it with as many people as you can! Don?t think of it in terms of getting a competitive advantage for yourself. That is the old, myopic vision of self-interest. The more people become educated and know about these things, the more they can help in solving the challenges that we all face. Happiness is found in sharing, and sharing leads to incredible discoveries. I see a day, not so far way, when people will be judged not by their ability to outsmart others, but by their ability to help others. Not by their ability to be the best students, but by their ability to be the best teachers.

That?s a world truly worth living in!

18.4 GROW YOUR OWN FOOD

This one is so obvious it almost makes me feel stupid to say it. Food is a form of energy, possibly the most important form of energy. It?s what our body runs on. But it?s also a form of power. Growing your own food is not just a leisure activity, or a hobby. It?s about taking the power back into your own hands. Roger Doiron calls this a *Subversive Plot*, one that instead of being about secrecy promotes openness and sharing. It?s a plot that does not benefit the few at the expenses of the many, but one that empowers each individual, and when we put all together we are all safer, healthier, and more independent. There are several advantages in keeping a personal garden, I will just list a few of them here.

- **Improve your health (and your family's).** Studies have shown that most of our illnesses are caused by bad diets and bad food. Not only is eating more fresh fruits and vegetables is one of the most important things you can do to stay healthy, but if you grow them yourself your children are twice as likely to eat healthier as well.[186]

- **Save money.** This goes without saying. Food prices have gone up significantly in the last years, and are likely to go up in the future. Why? Because it takes at least 10 calories of oil (equivalent) for each calorie of food we produce. Oil prices have gone up, and they can only go up from now on. Homegrown food can be an excellent supplement to your groceries, and in a typical family of four you can save up to $3,000 or more (the exact amount depends on a variety of factors).

- **Reduce your environmental impact**. This may not be of interest to all of you, but it should be. Consider that the ecosystems are all connected, and we all depend upon them. Even if you do not care about the environment per se, you should at least know that neglecting it will eventually hit you in the face. Try not to use chemical pesticides and fertilisers, there are many internet websites with great guides on how to use natural systems at their best, with minimum effort and maximum results (see permaculture), even if you live in the city (urban agriculture, hydroponics/aquaponics gardens).

- **Enjoy outdoor life**. Planting, weeding, watering, and harvesting are a great way to get some physical activity. Gardening also helps you relax and have time to think or let your mind wonder.

- **Community and family time**. Having a garden is a rewarding activity. It can be a great way to spend some time with your kids, and do something useful at the same time. Likewise, if you have friends who do not have a backyard and cannot grow their own food, share your garden! It will also give you a chance to share your produce with your neighbours, help each other out, and start rebuilding a sense of community.

- **Enjoy food that tastes better**. The freshest food you can have is that one that you pick yourself. When you go to the supermarket, the food that hit the shelves has been produced far away, harvested, packed, shipped, moved via trucks, airplanes, trains, boats, containers (oil, oil, oil). How long has it been sitting there before you picked it up? A day? A week? A month? Where has it been exactly? Where was it stored? What did they put in to make it look so flawless (and often tasteless)? Believe me, when you grab that fruit or veggie that you grew yourself and take a good juicy bite, you will know that you made the right choice.

- **Stop being a slave to the food companies**. Need I say more?

18.5   EAT LESS MEAT

This point is often misunderstood, as it carries a lot of emotional baggage, both from the pro and the against-meat side of the debate. I do not want to pick either. I am making a purely analytical statement based on simple physics and biology.

The physics. Producing lots of meat and using it as the primary source of food is highly inefficient. Intensive livestock production requires large quantities of harvested feed. According to the Food and Agriculture Organisation (FAO), "Ranching-induced deforestation is one of the main causes of loss of some unique plant and animal species in the tropical rain forests of Central and South America as well as carbon release in the atmosphere.'? It further states that "Expanding livestock production is one of the main drivers of the destruction of tropical rain forests in Latin America, which is causing serious environmental degradation in the region.'? An earlier FAO study found that 90% of deforestation is caused by unsustainable agricultural practices. Logging and plantation forestry, though not as major contributors to deforestation, play a greater role in forest degradation.[187]

Raising animals for human consumption accounts for approximately 40% of the total amount of agricultural output in industrialised countries today and livestock is the world's largest land user. Grazing occupies 26% of the earth's ice-free terrestrial surface, and feed crop production uses about one third of all arable land.[188] At a global scale, it has been estimated that livestock contribute, directly and indirectly, to about 9% of total anthropogenic carbon dioxide emissions, 37% of methane emissions and 65% of nitrous oxide emissions.[189] Just to give you a sense of the proportions involved, the production of 1 kg of wheat requires about 1 tonne of water. To produce to same amount of beef, we need more than 15 tonnes of water.[190] Not to mention other negative externalities of meat production, such as the loss of biodiversity and loss of local livestock breeds, the production and dissemination of antibiotic-resistant and pathogenic bacteria in animals and food, the release of naturally-occurring and synthetic hormones, ectoparasiticides and derivatives, the accumulation of heavy metals, and persistent organic pollutants.

The biology. Excessive meat consumption (particularly red meat) has been linked to many health problems, such as colon cancer,[191] oesophageal, lung, pancreatic and endometrial cancer,[192] breast cancer,[193] stomach cancer,[194] lymphoma,[195] bladder cancer,[196] lung cancer,[197] various cardiovascular diseases,[198] diabetes,[199] obesity,[200] hypertension and arthritis.[201]

I think that is quite enough.

The conclusion. Does this mean we should all become vegan? No. From the ethical perspective there is an intense debate going on which people will hold different views on, so I will leave it at that. Furthermore, even given the evidence above, there is absolutely no consensus around the fact that 'meat is bad' per se. The physical and biological evidence simply suggests that overproduction and overconsumption of meat is not such a great idea. Then, in addition to the physical reality, there is also the human aspect. Many people like to eat meat. Lots of delicacies in cuisines from all around the world have meat in their dishes. Should we be expected to willingly (or worse, forcefully) cast all of that aside and start living the vegan way? I propose a more common sense approach. Why don?t we try to just reduce meat consumption? It puts less strain on the environment, and it is healthier for us. You do not have to abandon meat altogether, just try not to eat it 14 times per week. Maybe start with 10, then eventually go to 5, or 2. See how it goes. Experiment. It does not have to feel like a sacrifice. Just try it out, and if you really cannot live without two meals of meat a day, then so be it. If, on the other hand, you find yourself living just as well, but with half or a fraction of the amount of meat you used to consume, then even better! You will live healthier, help the environment, and save some money too!

18.6   HUNGRY, HUNGRY, HOUSES (SAVE ENERGY)

When people talk about energy problems and their solutions these days, they associate it with renewable energy. The widespread idea is that the only problem is the source (hydrocarbon, which is very limited and takes a long time to form), and that if we just switched to solar, wind, geothermal, hydro, biomass, biofuel, tidal, or wave (which are renewable) then we would all be OK.

It is a bit like saying that if a barrel is leaking water because it has more holes than Swiss cheese, the solution is to pump more water in.

Making energy from renewable resources in your own house is great, but before you even start thinking about that, you should take care of big elephant in the room. Most of the energy we use is actually wasted. And I am not talking about the kids keeping the lights on around the house (although it?s better not to do that). Yes, we should not waste tap water when brushing our teeth, but compare that to the amount of *drinkable water* we waste every time we flush the toilet and the teeth-cleaning saving looks just laughable. Energy is wasted in heating, bad insulation systems, old appliances, bad designs, bad habits, and most of all *bad thinking*. Why would you install 10kw of solar photovoltaics, when you could retrofit your house *first*, and *then* need only a fraction of those?

Buildings are the ultimate end-users for 68% of coal and 55% of natural gas in the United States. There is a huge opportunity to mitigate fossil fuel consumption in this sector, and it has yet to be exploited. Also, consider that energy is not just electricity or oil. Water is energy, and by cutting your water consumption in half you need half the amount of gas to heat, half the electricity to move the pumps. We do not think about it in that way, but everything is connected, and everything that moves needs energy. *Ceteris paribus*, retrofitting is *always* cheaper and more efficient than simply switching to another source of energy. That means it has a greater return of investment, it costs less, and saves more. There are a million things you do, but here are just a few:

Figure 18.1: A comic strip I did back in 2009 for Blog Action Day.

- **LED lightbulbs**. They are less energy hungry, they do not contain toxic chemicals, and they last longer. And for those who love the yellowish "old style" feeling, they come in colours, too.

- **High efficiency household appliances**. In the EU they have classes A++ and A+++, in the United States they are certified by the Energy Star. They really save a lot of energy.

- **Programmable thermostats** that make use of Artificial Intelligence software. These beauties can save up to 50% of your annual consumption (the Nest is a good example of such a system.[202]).

- **Hot water heater 'blanket'**. Newer heaters have relatively high insulation, so to see if an Insulation Blanket is right for you, just put your hand on the outside of the heater. If it feels warm, then you can save money by wrapping it.[203]

- **Standby power reduction**. Save money with a few 'smart' power strips for your electronics where it is convenient. They automatically sense the sleep mode, shut off phantom loss and also shut off any 'associated' electronics that you plug into the same strip.[204]

- **Reduce water** use by installing aerators and low-flow shower heads (again, another 50% savings).

A conservative estimate says that the tuneups listed above have an average payback time of one year or less, a return of investment of 100%, and when combined can give you annual savings of more than a $1,000. That is, every year. And with rising costs of electricity, gas, and water, savings can only increase.

You can get creative and find many other ideas, and there is a plethora of websites run by enthusiasts dedicated to home retrofitting. Green And Save has an excellent table with all kinds of retrofitting (tuneups, remodelling, advanced systems), complete with payback time, added cost, annual savings, 10-year savings, and return of investment.[205] Then, if you want to get serious you can do deep energy retrofitting that makes use of integrative design[206], starting with insulating your walls, roof, basements, ducts, and replacing windows. This can take more time and money upfront, but it will prove itself in the long run, not just in saving but also in the quality of your home.

Remember that you do not have to do everything at once, and you do not have to do everything. Be smart and make use of the right technologies according to your living and environmental conditions, your house design, and your habits. According to the Green and Save simulation, if you did all the tune-ups, remodelling and advanced systems retrofitting, for an investment cost of $86,000 you can save up to $300,000 in 20 years. Of course your house will be slightly different, and you might want to choose to do only a few fixes, but it gives you a sense of proportion. Table 18.1 is a summary of the Return of Investment Tables.

Green Tune-ups				
Payback Time	Added cost	Annual savings	10-year savings	ROI
1.2 years	$1,320	$1,136	$11,360	96.5%

Green remodel				
Payback Time	Added cost	Annual savings	10-year savings	ROI
4.2 years	$15,814	$4,348	$43,480	26.8%

Green advanced systems				
Payback Time	Added cost	Annual savings	20-year savings	ROI
8.7 years	$69,590	$7,309	$182,170	11.8%

Table 18.1: Summary of house retrofit savings.

18.7   MAKE YOUR OWN ENERGY

Energy independence used to be very hard. Today, it seems like a crime not doing it. While the cost of fossil fuels has gone up, the cost of renewable technologies has drastically fallen.

Solar is already cheaper than nuclear[207], and in some places (like Italy and Spain) it will become cheaper than oil starting next year, possibly even without incentives[208] (with incentives this becomes an even easier task[209]). Solar is an exponentially growing technology, where we consistently observe a drop in costs and a rise in efficiency.[210] Depending on where you live, hot water solar panels have a payback time of 4-10 years, photovoltaics of 6-12 years, and hot air collectors of 1-2 years. Consider that these technologies operate at a minimum of 80% their original efficiency up until 30 years of use (they have a warranty), but even after that period *they still work*, just slightly less efficiently. Also, solar photovoltaics drop in cost by about half every two years, it already became incredibly cheap compared to what it was just five years ago, and it will continue to improve.

There are heat pumps, wind turbines, various systems of microgeneration and a myriad of technologies available to help you generate the energy you need. But remember, that has to be the last step of the way. **Energy saving should be your first priority, energy production comes afterwards**.

The most important form of energy is that of our brains. Use it wisely.

18.8   DITCH THE CAR

Having a car is convenient. You can use it whenever you want, move around with ease, do long trips, go to work, hang around with friends. Life would not be the same without a car. If you live in a rural area, you do not really have a choice, as without a car you are stuck in the middle of nowhere. However, if you live in the city (most people do), owning a car may be more of a hassle than a convenience. Here are a few reasons why you should consider not owning a car:

- **Saving money**. You may associate the cost of the car with the cost of gas prices. Given that they rise every single day, just this fact should make you wonder if keeping a car is really worth it, but in fact there are many other things to consider. Payment, repair, maintenance, insurance, depreciation... the true cost of owning a car is something between $5,000 and $15,000 annually (depending on the car, the location, and its usage).[211] That?s a lot of money. Think about how much you could save by using a combination of public transport, bicycle, walking, and the occasional car rental whenever needed.

- **Reduce accidents**. If you tried to license a technology that injures 1.6 million people and kills another 40,000 every year in Europe alone, they'd never let you open your business. Yet that is exactly what car accidents do.[212] Things will change when self-driving cars become ubiquitous, but then again, by that time almost nobody will need to own a car. Why go through all the hassle, when you can just call the closest automated car with your cellphone, hop in, and let it drive you around? Payments can be done automatically with the phone, cars will be operating at maximum efficiency, at a fraction of the cost.

- **Cleaner air**. Until we switch to fully electric cars, powered by all-renewable energies, cars will pollute. The more people use them, the less liveable the city is.It?s as simple as that.

- **Rediscover your community**. Research has shown a direct correlation between the amount of traffic on a street and the number of neighbours people know by name. The fewer cars there are, the more likely people are to spend time outside their front doors. If you want to get to know people in your area, walk.[213]

- **Avoid traffic and stress**. Particularly useful in rush hours, using a bike can save you a considerable amount of time, not to mention stress.

- **Be healthier**. In 2010, the CDC reported higher numbers once more, counting 35.7% of American adults as obese, and 17% of American children.[214] As of February 2012 experts predict that over half the United States population will be obese in just 3 years compared to a 1/3 of the United Kingdom who could be obese by 2020.[215] Walking, cycling, running, skating, whatever you decide, will make you healthier. Not just that, but you will be saving a hell of a lot of money in health care (medicines, visits, surgery and who knows what as a consequence of neglecting your body). ou might not even need to go to the gym, which again saves you more money.

If you really need a car for special circumstances, you can always resort to carsharing, a very popular system that is growing rapidly around the world. *Carsharing* is different from a typical rental services and offers many advantages, as it is not limited by office hours; reservation, pickup, and return is all self-service; vehicles can be rented by the minute, by the hour, as well as by the day; locations are distributed throughout the service area, and often located for access by public transportation; insurance and fuel costs are included in the rates. Many parallel system have evolved out of this idea, such as *peer-to-peer* car rental system in Germany, The Netherlands, the UK, the US, Canada, Spain, and Slovenia.[216]

Of course there is the good old *carpooling*, which is now much easier thanks to the Internet and mobile apps. There are many websites that help you find a ride, you can even choose the kind of person you would like to share the car with, based on your tastes in music, movies, art, or sports. And, why not, you could even find your partner in this way!

CHAPTER 19

MAKING THE FUTURE

"The best way to predict the future is to create it."

– Peter F. Drucker [217]

It used to be the case that great social change could come from the minds and determination of extraordinary individuals. Then everything changed. After the second industrial revolution, as societies increased in complexity, larger and larger investments were required to invent, experiment, and distribute the fruits of one's ideas – until the amount of money necessary for making anything non-trivial happen became so massively gargantuan that only large corporations could afford it.

Today, we are on the verge of a new industrial revolution, one that takes the power back to the people – the makers, the hackers, the industrious inventors and creators that are quickly shaping the future. It is the emergence of the DIY (Do It Yourself) community of innovators that are building the physical, digital, and cultural tools for a new society. These silent heroes often do not have a name, or a face, but we are collectively eating the fruits of their work every day. And we can do so because they are building new things, writing code, creating beautiful works of art, and releasing them under Free/Open Source licences.

I believe we are at the dawn of a new civilisation.

19.1   SUPPORT OPEN SOURCE PROJECTS

Whenever I utter the words "Open Source", people either do not know what they mean, or they think about software. "Isn't that like the Linux thing?". Sure. Linux, GNU, and thousands of other projects are Free and Open Source, but they are just an infinitesimal part of the whole.

Open Source is not just software. It is a philosophy. It?s the idea that sharing is better than secrecy. It?s the proof that cooperation is more effective than ruthless

135

competition; and that by opening up the blueprints, the development of science, culture, the arts, and everything that is positive accelerates. It is possibly the most outstanding example of all human achievements, the light in the tunnel of our gloomy idiosyncrasies, a triumph of transcendence from our primitive condition. It is what gives me hope for the future of humanity, the reason I think we can evade the path of self-destruction, and move forward as a species.

Over the past 30 years, the Open Source philosophy has pervaded every aspect of our lives, and everything it has touched has been made better. It is an inconceivable force, inspiring millions of people to create positive change in the world. What may have started as 'just software'[218] moved on to virtually every other field of science, the arts, and even our culture at large. We have open hardware (e.g. Arduino, a microcontroller platform for hobbyists, artists and designers), open beverages (Open Cola and Open Beer!), open books, open films, open robotics, open design, open journalism, and even experiments of open governance.[219]

Open Source pioneer Linus Torvalds, father of Linux, famously said:[220]

"The future is Open Source everything."

In order to understand what this means, we need to look no further than the pages of this very book you are holding right now. The development of '*Robots will steal your job, but that is OK: how to survive the economic collapse and be happy*' was possible thanks to a crowdfunding campaign that I launched on a website. The software used to write the book was mostly Free and Open Source (FOSS), running on an operating system which heavily relies on FOSS to work.[221] The very browser you used to find my book is probably FOSS, too. Google Chrome, Firefox, Safari, they are all FOSS. But also Wikipedia, Creative Commons, many Flickr photos and videos on YouTube and Vimeo are released under some sort of free/open licenses. More recently, there has been a wave of Open Source projects covering an incredibly broad spectrum, even including physical objects such as flashlights, sensors, bicycles, solar panels, and 3D printers.

Internet communities such as IndieGoGo and Kickstarter are great places to start directly supporting Open Source projects that will help us to live a better life. The concept is simple. Somebody has a great idea that they would like to develop, they share it with the community and ask for a certain amount of money to complete or to continue the project. People who are interested pitch in, and get rewards for that. Over 90% of the money goes to the original artist/inventor, but what they create benefits the whole community. Many choose to release the source code/technical specifics to the public, Open Source.

This is a great way to support *what* you like, *how* you like. You can choose which projects to support, and the amount of money you want to pledge. It gives you a sense of fulfilment and power. It makes you feel part of a community of like-minded people. And most of all, it is *fair*. There are no under-the-table-games, no special interests, no bribing of government officials. It?s meritocracy at its best.

To put things in perspective, Kickstarter is on track to distribute over $150 million dollars to its users' projects in 2012, or more than the entire fiscal year 2012 budget for the National Endowment of the Arts (NEA), which was $146 million.[222]

We cannot expect governments to solve all of our problems. Of course, it would be nice if public money were spent wisely and on programmes that helped everyone, operating at maximum efficiency. But we all know that as much as we try, this often remains only wishful thinking. We must not lose faith in our governments completely, but we should not wait and pretend that some day everything will be magically fixed. We must take things in our own hands, and accelerate positive change.

My advice is to provide as much support as you can to Open Source projects that are fundamental to the development of humanity, such as Wikipedia, Creative Commons, The Electronic Frontier Foundation, as well as many micro projects of your interest. Whatever you can donate will help. $50, $20, or even $1 can make the difference. It will not only help out the creator and the community at large, but also you directly. If you can reduce your dependence on money by utilising something that was created through an Open Source project, which you helped co-fund, you are in a satisfying position. Once something goes Open Source, it is available to the entire human race, forever. It is a win-win situation.

Now, to a more pragmatic approach. I can imagine you thinking "Yeah, this is all very nice, but I can't live off Wikipedia". Actually, I would object even to that (inexhaustible source of knowledge and references), but I get what you mean. Physical stuff? Things that you can use to live? Right. I will just give you one example, but there are many.

Marcin Jakubowski is an incredible man. There are plenty of people who talk about building a better world. Many have great ideas, too, futuristic visions of how the world could be, if we just wanted to. But one of them is actually building it. His goal: no less than creating a post-scarcity society, where people have to work only 1-2 hours per day to live, so that they can use the remaining time for higher purposes. He is building the foundation for the next paradigm in social evolution, and he is open-sourcing all of it. A visionary, but with solid grounding. The story is best told by Marcin himself, who spoke at TED in 2011. This talk has been watched more than 1.5 million times and it was translated in 41 languages.[223]

"I started a group called Open Source Ecology. We've identified the 50 most important machines that we think it takes for modern life to exist – things from tractors, bread ovens, circuit makers. Then we set out to create an Open Source, DIY, do it yourself version that anyone can build and maintain at a fraction of the cost. We call this the Global Village Construction Set.

So let me tell you a story. I finished my 20s with a Ph.D. in fusion energy, and I discovered I was useless. I had no practical skills. The world presented me with options, and I took them. I guess you can call it the consumer lifestyle. So I started a farm in Missouri and learned about the economics of farming. I bought a tractor – then it broke. I paid to get it repaired – then it broke again. Then pretty soon, I was broke too.

I realised that the truly appropriate, low-cost tools that I needed to start a sustainable farm and settlement just did not exist yet. I needed tools that were robust, modular, highly efficient and optimised, low-cost, made from local and recycled materials that would last a lifetime, not designed for obsolescence. I found that I would have to build them myself. So I did just that. And I tested them. And I found that industrial productivity can be achieved on a small scale.

So then I published the 3D designs, schematics, instructional videos and budgets on a wiki. Then contributors from all over the world began showing up, prototyping new machines during dedicated project visits. So far, we have prototyped eight of the 50 machines. And now the project is beginning to grow on its own.

We know that Open Source has succeeded with tools for managing knowledge and creativity. And the same is starting to happen with hardware too. We're focusing on hardware because it is hardware that can change people's lives in such tangible material ways. If we can lower the barriers to farming, building, manufacturing, then we can unleash just massive amounts of human potential.

That's not only in the developing world. Our tools are being made for the American farmer, builder, entrepreneur, maker. We've seen lots of excitement from these people, who can now start a construction business, parts manufacturing, organic CSA or just selling power back to the grid. Our goal is a repository of published designs so clear, so complete, that a single burned DVD is effectively a civilisation starter kit.

I have planted a hundred trees in a day. I have pressed 5,000 bricks in one day from the dirt beneath my feet and built a tractor in six days. From what I have seen, this is only the beginning.

If this idea is truly sound, then the implications are significant. A greater distribution of the means of production, environmentally sound supply chains, and a newly relevant DIY maker culture can hope to transcend artificial scarcity. We're exploring the limits of what we all can do to make a better world with open hardware technology."

Together, we can begin to transition towards of society of openness that benefits all, instead of one of secrecy that serves the powerful. Author Clay Shirky pointed out that Wikipedia represents the cumulation of 100 million hours of human thought. With 100 million hours of thought and collaboration we were able to create the largest and most complete encyclopaedia of all time, *"a world in which every single person on the planet is given free access to the sum of all human knowledge. That's what we're doing"*.[224] Compare that to television watching. Two hundred billion hours of television is watched, in the U.S. alone, every year. Put another way, we have 2,000 Wikipedia projects a year spent watching television, and 100 million hours (1 Wikipedia project) every weekend, simply watching the ads.[225]

Just think about what we could achieve if we were able to capture even a fraction of that time and use it for something useful. The possibilities are endless – together we can create a truly wonderful world.

It has already begun. Join in ☺

19.2   VOTE WITH YOUR WALLET (NOT WHAT YOU THINK)

We know that politics is largely influenced by big businesses, which have the power to lobby extensively. As far as I am concerned voting does not happen in the voting booth as much as it happens at the mall. If you think about it, you effectively have more voting power when you decide to buy something, because you influence businesses in their strategies, which in turn has an effect on politics. If there is one thing corporations understand it is profit, and more specifically the loss of profit. Walmart did not start its eco-business because they had a change of heart; suddenly wanting to help the environment, providing people healthier foods and better products. They did it because they saw a market there, a shift in interest from the public. If there is a market somewhere, somebody will fill that gap. Essentially, you really are voting with your wallet, every day of your life, you just didn?t notice.

Next time you go to the mall and pick something up, ask yourself if you really need it. Will it just give you temporary satisfaction, or will it really serve you well? Do you really need that 20th pair of jeans? What about the other 19? Are they not good enough? Then why did you buy them? Or did you like them at first, but then quickly changed your mind?

Get rid of things you do not need. Sell them on eBay, at the street market, give them away as presents, it doesn?t matter. Buy smart (more on this later), and stop being a slave to the corporate machine, take back control over your life. They want us to think that freedom is the liberty to choose between two hundred brands of toothpaste.

Taste real freedom!

19.3   WORK LESS, BE SELF-EMPLOYED

Go back and have a glance at the last thirty pages or so. You might have noticed that they all had something in common. They were ideas on how to save money, but without having to sacrifice the things you liked. In fact, they might even help you to live healthier, less stressed, and happier lives. Add everything up and you will see that by following this advice you can save several thousands of dollars every year. This is money that you used to need, but you don?t anymore. So what can you do with this extra money? You can be smart and spend it on things you will actually enjoy (see the chapter on how to spend smart), or you could be even smarter and see this as an opportunity to work less. That's right. If you need less money, why not go part-time? Why not change job and do something that you *really* like, but that does not pay as much as the other (less satisfying) job? Having lessened the need for money in the first place, reducing the workweek could be the first step towards a more fulfilling and less stressful life.

This should be obvious by now, and it is not a radical idea. A group of economists at the British think tank New Economics Foundation (NEF) has re-commended moving to a shorter workweek, publishing a report outlining the motivations and the general plan: "A 'normal' working week of 21 hours could help to address a range of urgent, interlinked problems: overwork, unemployment, over-consumption, high carbon emissions, low well-being, entrenched inequalities, and the lack of time to live sustainably, to care for each other, and simply to enjoy life".[226]

The report continues:

> "A much shorter working week would change the tempo of our lives, reshape habits and conventions, and profoundly alter the dominant cultures of western society. Arguments for a 21-hour week fall into three categories, reflecting three interdependent 'economies', or sources of wealth, derived from the natural resources of the planet,

from human resources, assets and relationships, inherent in everyone's everyday lives, and from markets. Our arguments are based on the premise that we must recognise and value all three economies and make sure they work together for sustainable social justice.

Safeguarding the natural resources of the planet. Moving towards a much shorter working week would help break the habit of living to work, working to earn, and earning to consume. People may become less attached to carbon-intensive consumption and more attached to relationships, pastimes, and places that absorb less money and more time. It would help society to manage without carbon-intensive growth, release time for people to live more sustainably, and reduce greenhouse gas emissions.

Social justice and well-being for all. A 21-hour 'normal' working week could help distribute paid work more evenly across the population, reducing ill-being associated with unemployment, long working hours and too little control over time. It would make it possible for paid and unpaid work to be distributed more equally between women and men; for parents to spend more time with their children – and to spend that time differently; for people to delay retirement if they wanted to, and to have more time to care for others, to participate in local activities and to do other things of their choosing. Critically, it would enable the 'core' economy to flourish by making more and better use of unmodified human resources in defining and meeting individual and shared needs. It would free up time for people to act as equal partners, with professionals and other public service workers, in co-producing well-being.

A robust and prosperous economy. Shorter working hours could help to adapt the economy to the needs of society and the environment, rather than subjugating society and environment to the needs of the economy. Business would benefit from more women entering the workforce; from men leading more rounded, balanced lives; and from reductions in work-place stress associated with juggling paid employment and home-based responsibilities. It could also help to end credit-fueled growth, to develop a more resilient and adaptable economy, and to safeguard public resources for investment in a low-carbon industrial strategy and other measures to support a sustainable economy."

Such an economy, one that approaches the steady-state advocated by Herman Daly and others, would also have the great value of being resilient and adaptable. There are many necessary conditions to achieve before the 21-hour workweek can be put into practice, and the report outlines a transition with lucidity and valuable insight. Simply reducing the workweek, ceteris paribus, could potentially backfire, as we have seen in previous experiments (France 2000-2008), there needs to be some adjustments to go along with it. People need time to adapt, so there should be a transitional period that lasts a few years, a guaranteed fair income, social norms and expectations must change, not to mention gender relationship. But above all, the overall culture must change. People need to see the *merit* and the *need* for a different system, so that they themselves will ask for it, instead of resisting it.

My advice to you would be to *make a plan that, over the course of a few years, will allow you to transition towards a reduced workweek, or to a job that pays less but gives you more satisfaction.* Escaping the labour-for-income trap is not an easy task, and should be taken seriously, or else you might find yourself in a very uncomfortable situation (especially if you have a family that depends on you for living). Use the resources in this book, begin exploring the new possibilities, and don?t be afraid to ask for help from your friends, family, or even strangers. Once you begin to open up yourself to a different way of living, you will find whole communities of people willing to give advice.

This is your life. Live it to its fullest!

19.4   DON'T BE A DICK

This is a largely overlooked aspect of the world of activism. I have been involved with non-profit organisations and social movements for a long time. Having started a few of them myself, I know how painful it can be for those who are not active members to have somebody school them about how they should live their lives. There is nothing more infuriating than being told that everything you have been doing for your whole life is wrong, and that you should change it. Even if that were true – and is many cases is not – it still would be the wrong approach in getting them to join you.

First of all, it is a horrible communication strategy. Very few people are open-minded enough to challenge their own beliefs and the habits that have accompanied them for their entire lives, and discard them in a few seconds. And even in the rare event when that happens, it could have been achieved much more efficiently by utilising a different strategy, rather than making them feeling guilty and inadequate. It is hard enough to get by these days, the last thing people need is for some bourgeois self-righteous environmentalist to climb up the pedestal and start lecturing you. If you want people to join you, you must show *the value* of what you are proposing, and you must lead by example. I know, action is a lot harder than talking about stuff, and sometimes you may be overwhelmed by the events around you. It cannot be helped, we are inside a system, and in some way we have to work with the tools we have at our disposal to transition towards a better society. That, or isolating yourself from the rest of the world. I think the latter is a rather myopic and selfish way of responding to the problem, so I will focus on the former option.

We are running out of time, but that is no reason for hurrying and making a mess of things. Instead, we need to realise that we must find the most efficient and effective way in transitioning to the new system. Before you do anything, ask yourself the question: how effective is it? Think about the issue of meat consumption. Most vegans I know are quite vocal about their choice, and if that was the whole story it would not be much of an issue. The problem is that some of them are obnoxiously arrogant and violent in their approach. Those who disagree with them are seen as murderers, or looked upon with contempt, sometimes even disgust. Just by looking at vegan activists leaflets and websites you can spot the obvious scare tactics, trying to exploit the empathy of the viewer and spark an emotional reaction. If the goal is to scare, outrage, and distance people from you, this is certainly an effective way to achieve just that. If, on the other hand, your goal is to make people more conscious and aware of a particular problem, you might want to start by respecting them, and showing the merits of your way of living.

Again, ask yourself, is it easier to convert 10% of the people to eat no meat at all, or is it easier to convince 50% to eat less meat? The answer is very simple, and the concept is well developed by Graham Hill in his short book *Weekday Vegetarian: Finally, a Palatable Solution* and TED Talk *Why I'm a weekday vegetarian.*[227] Imagine yourself being committed to the cause. At some point, you will look at your last hamburger, or your last steak, and you will know that you will not be having any more of those, forever. Many people are not quite ready for that. So what if you were to start a more gradual, easier approach? A weekday vegetarian seems like a more reasonable and palatable solution, one that most people would be willing to adopt, without having to drastically and dramatically change their habits. Yet, by cutting meat to only once or twice per week, you would have essentially reduced your meat consumption by 70-80%.

The same line of thinking works for every aspect of our lives. It is very difficult to be 100% consistent with your values, but you can strive for an honest, non-hypocritical way of living, without making yourself unbearable to live with.

CHAPTER 20

HOW TO BE HAPPY

During my research, I spent a great deal of time reading books from the self help category. I travelled to twenty countries, spent thousands of dollars on seminars, dug deep into the abyss of happiness, so that you don?t have to.

So here is the moment you have all been waiting for, the very reason you bought this book. I am going to give you the definitive and final secret to happiness. A secret that has been kept for millennia, passed on from genius to genius, from Leonardo Da Vinci to Albert Einstein, now finally to be revealed. Ready? Here it is.

If something is going wrong with your life, it is because you are sending out negative vibrations, which then come back to you amplified. So you should force yourself to think positively all the time.

- Change your thoughts, change your life, change the Universe.

- Changing your habits. Eat better, get more exercise. All these things will have a snowball effect and your life will take a dramatic shift in the positive direction.

- If you want to be rich and famous, think and act like a rich and famous person. Buy first class tickets on the plane, surround yourself with rich people. You will become one of them sooner than you think.

I believe it is called quantum mechanics. Or something. Oh wait, or was it vibrations? Yeah, that sounds better. Vibrations. Quantum vibrations! That must be it.[228]

OK, let us be serious now. While I enjoy picking on the self-help idiocy wave that has invaded the United States and the UK over the last few years, there are some suggestions that might actually help you, if you approach them with a bit of scientific rigour.

I imagine you must be pretty tired of reading about things that do not work, scientific analyses with no clear distinction between correlation and causation, and plain old common sense masqueraded as hidden truth. How about some practical suggestions, things that you can apply in your daily life, that you would not already know? You know my position regarding self-help. I think it is mostly a pseudoscientific scam that greedy people play on the desperate and the gullible. However, if taken seriously, there are some things you could try, and that might actually help you live a happier life. Please note that you should not take this advice as a unidirectional to do list, or as an instruction manual that you just have to follow, and everything will magically fix itself. The following is an organic, evolving and ever-changing list, the result of rigorous scientific experiments, tested on large groups of people over long periods of time, and that consistently show a pattern.[229] This does not mean that they will work for everyone, at all moments of their lives. But it is better than nothing or pseudoscientific mumbo jumbo. Remember that these are not rules, they are advice. They are not instructions, they are suggestions. Be smart.

I cannot promise you happiness, but I can promise to present you only the things that research shows to be effective, and that *I also tried myself*, first hand. This is the closest I will get to a "self-help guide". Actually, see it more of a set of suggestions on how to go about creating lasting positive change, but with the benefit of the doubt. Try them yourself, at your own pace, without stress. With that in mind, let us begin.

20.1 LIVE SMART

Mindfulness Meditation

Contrary to what many self-help positive psychology books might want you to believe, pushing aside bad memories and sad thoughts, trying to replace them only with the happy, even forcing yourself to do so, does not work. Instead, take some time every day for yourself to let your mind roam free. Find a quiet spot, turn off the cell phone, close your eyes, breath slowly, and try to relax. This will allow your body and mind to create connections and learn from the overwhelming amount of stimuli that you are constantly exposed to.

Write down things that need resolution

It does not really matter if you actually come up with solutions (although it would be best if you did), the act of externalising the problems you think you are facing helps you focus and put them in perspective. Typically, we tend to overestimate the importance or the effect that certain events have in our lives, and let our unrestricted feelings be the driver of our mood. This way you can approach things more rationally.

Write down the good things that happened to you today

Small things matter, even if we tend to let them pass by. At the end of the day, take a moment and think about three things for which you are grateful, three good things that you did, or that happened to you today. Please note that you are not forcing yourself to be happy or to only have happy thoughts, you are just reminding yourself to recall the happy things that you might otherwise forget. As you step down the hedonic treadmill, you will learn to appreciate life a little more, and put yourself in a good mood while doing it.

Exercise

Our body is an extension of our mind. The nervous system stretches out to our arms, legs, muscles. Experimental evidence shows that people who exercise are happier than those who do not (in controlled conditions). You do not have to take expensive courses or do extreme sports. Start with something simple, even a 10-20 minute run will do. If you can, take the bike instead of the car. In time, you will begin to notice that it will make you feel better (and you will gain in physical shape, too).

In fact, there is a plethora of studies that show walking as nature's best medicine. It appears that simply walking at least 30 minutes per day is the single best thing you can do for your health.[230] If you can limit sitting and sleeping to 23 and 1/2 hours per day or less, you are on the right track to be healthier and happier.

Random acts of kindness

Research shows that people helping others reported increased levels of happiness. Imagine you find a $10 bill on the street. If you spend that money for yourself, you will be much less happy than you would have been, had you spent it for someone else. Buy your friends a cup of coffee, a dinner, a concert ticket to their favourite band. But random acts of kindness need not to be necessarily monetary. They could take the form of a handmade present. An unexpected phone call to a distant friend, or to a relative you rarely see. A song performed with friends. Big or small, it does not matter. The two crucial aspects are: randomness and kindness. If you start giving a present every month to your partner, they will get used to receiving one which creates an expectation, which will then result in less happiness, and plain dissatisfaction when the present does not come, or when it feels cheap, not genuine. The unexpected nature of the act makes it more powerful, and the less they expect it, the greater the effect will be.

Cultivate new experiences

Following the same line as the previous point, trying new things will help you step down from the hedonic treadmill and hedonic adaptation trap. Again, they do not have to be big. If you are right handed, try brushing your teeth with your left hand. Going back home tonight, take a route you have never taken before. Taste a food you have never heard of. Try a new sport. Remember, don?t exaggerate any of this advice. Compulsively switching from one thing to another without taking a breath will not do you much good. Be balanced.

Set small, realistic goals

We like to dream big, and if our goal is particularly positive and fulfilling we will experience the sense of flow and drive that we talked about before. That?s all well and good, but we must not forget that life is made of many moments, and each one counts. Set yourself very small goals, even ridiculously easy goals, like a 1-minute run out of the blue. Remember when you were a child and you tried to avoid the imaginary river of lava, jumping from sofa to sofa? It is sort of the same thing. Drinking a glass of water? See if you can do it in five seconds. You have to finish a book soon? Try setting the goal of reading two pages before the hour. Two pages seems easy and effortless, so you just do it. Once you are in the mindset of reading, you are more likely to keep reading.

20.2   SPEND SMART

We have seen how earning above an income of $75,000 annually bears little to no relationship with your general happiness. That is because other factors kick in, like our personal relationships, family, friends, aspirations, dreams. But who said those are mutually exclusive things? A recent paper published in the Journal of Consumer Psychology explains just how "If money doesn't make you happy, then you probably aren't spending it right".[231] We tend to spend a lot of money on things that provide us with an ephemeral sense of instant satisfaction, instead of those that will make us happier. Our failure to predict the hedonic consequences of the future is one reason, coupled with the fact that very few approach the question of happiness with a scientific basis. We tend to rely on our gut feeling, which, as we have seen, is almost certainly wrong. The work conducted by Dan, Gilbert, and Wilson is impressive to say the least. It is the result of many years of thorough and meticulous research, and it references more papers than most of us could bear to read. So, if you do not feel like reading thousands of pages of scientific research, here is an 8-point summary that will help you get started.

Buy experiences instead of things

"Go out and buy yourself something nice" is the advice we often give to friends who just got some bad news; alas, it might be a very bad one. The pleasure as a result of the acquisition of material possession does not last very long. We get used to things pretty quickly. Things remain the same, and they are difficult to share. Experiences are different. They are as unique as the people who are having them. Experiences can be anticipated, lived, and then remembered. But most importantly, we can share experiences with other people, and other people – as we are now about to see – are our greatest source of happiness.

Help others instead of yourself

Human beings are the most social animals on this planet. We are the only species that creates complex social networks even with those who are not directly related with us. Spending money on ourselves makes us significantly less happy than spending it on other people. Be it on charity or on your friends, giving money away improves your general well-being. Even small amounts count, and even thinking about it helps, prosocial spending has a surprisingly powerful impact on social relationships.

Buy many small pleasures instead of few big ones

"Adaptation is a little bit like death: we fear it, fight it, and sometimes forestall it, but in the end, we always lose. And like death, there may be benefits to accepting its inevitability." Because we adapt to just about anything, few large purchases are really worth it; it is better to learn and savour the experience that comes from many small things. The more difficult it is to understand, explain, and thus adapt to a new situation, the more exciting it becomes. Small frequent pleasures are unpredictable, they surprise us, they are novel. Having a beer with friends after work is never the same as having the same beer with your girlfriend, but the kitchen table you bought last week stayed pretty much the same. Embrace the excitement of novelty and uncertainty of cultivating many small experiences.

Buy less insurance

If the bad news is that we adapt to good things, the good news is that we adapt to bad things as well. Virtually anything can happen to us, and over a year or less, it has little to no impact on our general well-being. It is like a psychological immune system, that protects us from bad experiences. Buying expensive extended warranties to guard against the loss of consumer goods may be unnecessary emotional protection. People seek extended warranties and generous return policies so as to prevent future regrets, but research suggests that the warranties may be unnecessary for happiness and the return policies could actually undermine it.

Pay now and consume later

Immediate gratification can lead you to make purchases you cannot afford, or may not even truly want. Impulse buying also deprives you of the distance necessary to make reasoned decisions. It eliminates any sense of anticipation, which is a strong source of happiness. Delaying consumption provides the benefit of anticipation, but it may also promote happiness in two other ways. First, it may alter what you choose (and you might make a better, more informed decision), second it may create uncertainty (which is again a good thing). For maximum happiness, savour (or even prolong!) the uncertainty of deciding whether to buy, what to buy, and the time waiting for the object of your desire to arrive.

Think about what you are not thinking about

When we consider a future purchase we tend to give extreme importance to features that have little to do with what will actually improve our experience once we acquire it. We look at major features, like how beautiful a house looks from the outside, instead of the little things that will actually impact our living there. We overestimate the importance of major features, whereas happiness lies in the little, everyday things. Before making a major purchase, consider the mechanics and logistics of owning this thing, and where your actual time will be spent once you own it. Try to imagine a typical day in your life, in some detail, hour by hour: how will it be affected by this purchase?

Beware of comparison shopping

One of the dangers of comparison shopping is that that the comparisons we make when we are shopping are not the same comparisons we will make when we consume what we shopped for. In other words, the reasons for which we buy something are not the reasons for which we will enjoy having that thing. Do not get tricked into comparing for the sake of comparison; try to weight only those criteria that actually matter to your enjoyment or the experience.

Follow the herd instead of your head

Do not overestimate your ability to independently predict how much you will enjoy something. We are, scientifically speaking, very bad at this. But if something reliably makes others happy, it is likely to make you happy, too. Thanks to the Internet we have a profusion of websites where people can review a purchase, and how much they enjoyed it. Weight other people's opinions and user reviews heavily in your purchasing decisions, picture yourself owning it and see how it could play out.

We know that money is not the cause of happiness, but it can be an enabler, if used correctly. Follow these eight steps before you decide to spend your money. That is, if you need to spend it at all!

CHAPTER 21

THE FUTURE IS BEAUTIFUL

One of my favourite films of all time is the philosophical oneiric adventure in rotoscope written and directed by Richard Linklater, Waking Life (2001).[232] This film has had a profound impact in my life and in the way I look at the world.

There is one scene in particular, which I think captures the essence of being alive, in light of the future to come, and I would like to share it with you.

Man on the Train: Hey, are you a dreamer?

Wiley: Yeah.

Man on the Train: I haven't seen too many around lately. Things have been tough lately for dreamers. They say dreaming is dead, no one does it anymore. It is not dead it is just that it is been forgotten, removed from our language. Nobody teaches it so nobody knows it exists. The dreamer is banished to obscurity. Well, I'm trying to change all that, and I hope you are too. By dreaming, every day. Dreaming with our hands and dreaming with our minds. Our planet is facing the greatest problems it is ever faced, ever. So whatever you do, don't be bored.

This simple, often forgotten, fact is even more true today. Since the dawn of human history, going back some 200 thousand years, we have gazed up at the stars, or looked into the fire and let our imagination run wild. Our evolved neocortex allowed us to develop language, abstract thought, and desires. We have transcended our condition, since we decided that we would not just stand by and passively accept the fate that the elements made for us. We were able to imagine a different world, a better future, and we had the power to make it a reality.

153

The world is a very big place, yet it is also quite small. It is our society – a complex organism, seemingly impossible to understand or control, yet a few simple but powerful ideas could change everything.

We are made to believe that our actions, what an individual does, cannot possibly hope to have an impact on millions, or even billions of people. For thousands of years, one could only hope to change a little bit history in the course of their entire life. Maybe you could impact a hundred, or a few thousand people at most. Today, the possibility exists for me to change for the better the lives of more people in ten years than anybody has ever done in human history. And so can you. This is a privilege that nobody had before. To think that we are the first generation to live this opportunity is exhilarating to say to least. It is electrifying. It is awe-inspiring. It is beautiful.

I want to leave you with the last sentence by the Man on the Train, speaking Linklater's mind, and my own:

> *"This is absolutely the most exciting time we could have possibly hoped to be alive. And things are just starting".*

HOW A FAMILY CAN LIVE BETTER BY
SPENDING SMART

In this book I outlined the various ways one can transition towards a better way a spending money, by downshifting. This is an example of the essential expenses that a fairly typical Italian family of four people has to sustain. Of course, families have different sizes, different needs, and in different countries that are different legislations, taxes, and hence costs. For example, in the United States taxes are paid after being paid, while in Italy and most of Europe they are detracted from the pay check (which covers most medical bills and other services offered by the state). I know, there are many differences, but I wanted to frame the problem – using real data – to give some perspective.

I took the data from my own family's 2011 expenses – a family of four (my parents, my brother, and my sister), living in northern Italy, middle class. I divided the expenses by category, and converted from Euros to US Dollars; the total came out to be $45,400. You can see the result in Table A.1. I have only listed the *essential expenses*, those that I think are necessary for a decent life.

At first glance we can immediately spot the outliers. Cars are the top expense – $15,000. I divided the expenses of the cars in leasing cost (average of $20,000 per car, spread over an average lifespan of 8 years),[233] and the annual costs of insurances, taxes, gasoline, maintenance and repair – about $7,500). My mother works nearby the house, so she happily takes the bike. My brother has many colleagues at work, and decides to car pool with them, sharing the cost of gasoline. We still need a car though, my father travels extensively, and generally speaking having at least one car is essential in the family.

Next, food is 'eating up' $12,000 a year. By growing our own food, we can save up to $3,000 (we have seen this in Chapter 18.4, *Grow Your Own Food*). The costs of electricity and gas ($2,000 and $3,000, respectively) can also be reduced by retrofitting.

Expense item	Annual cost ($)
Food	12,000
Electricity	2,000
Gas (heating and cooking)	3,000
Taxes (Property tax, Water, Waste)	1,000
House Insurance	700
3 Cars leasing	7,500
3 Cars (tax, insurance, gas, maintenance)	7,500
Clothing	3,000
Travel (train, bus)	2,000
Unexpected	3,000
Medical bills	3,700
Total	45,400

Table A.1: Approximate expense in 2011 of my family (four people).

On the other hand, travel costs have gone up – since we rely more on public transport and car-pooling.

Given the adjustments just mentioned, this is what the new table of costs looks like:

Expense item	Annual cost ($)
Food	9,000
Electricity	0
Gas (heating and cooking)	500
Taxes (Property tax, Water, Waste)	1,000
House Insurance	700
1 Car leasing	2,500
1 Car (tax, insurance, gas, maintenance)	2,500
Clothing	3,000
Travel (train, bus, car pooling)	3,000
Unexpected	3,000
Medical bills	3,700
Total	29,400

Table A.2: A projection of reduced expenses by spending smart.

Table A.2 shows the projection of reduced expenses. We are down to $29,400 from the initial sum of $45,400. Of course, this cannot be achieved in one year, retrofits and alternative energy sources can take anything from 3 months to 8 years to pay for themselves. We have to take this experiment for what it is – *a multi-year plan, not a quick fix that will magically solve everything.*

APPENDIX B

GROWTH

In his 2012 State of the Union Address, Barack Obama laid out a plan to 'put America back on its feet'. Almost all of the proposition had one common, basic assumption. If we want to get better, we need to 'grow the economy'. Every single policy that was proposed had as an underlining principle that economic growth through employment of labour is the driving force that will restore balance and make everyone happier.

Sounds reasonable? Every industrialised nation has experienced an increase in the quality of life of its citizens, thanks to economic growth. We have grown our way out of poverty, so to speak. We have gone from a primarily agrarian culture, to the unstoppable mechanical machine of mass production, which has globalised the planetary market. Economic growth has given us all the wonderful things that make our lives easier, and generally better. Roads, lights, trains, electricity, airplanes, running water in our houses, computers, cellphones, flatscreen TVs, the Internet, modern medicine. We have extended our lives by a factor of two in less than a century. Another way of putting it, economic growth not only made our lives more enjoyable, but also twice as long.

Good. Great. Fantastic! We should then follow this path indefinitely, it will solve all our problems, and we will always live better and better! Before we rush to conclusions, let us see for how long can we keep this up.

GROWTH AND ENERGY CONSUMPTION

"We were hunters and foragers. The frontier was everywhere. We were bounded only by the earth in the ocean and the sky. The open road still softly calls. Our little terraqueous globe is the madhouse of those hundred, thousand, millions of worlds. We who cannot even put our own planetary home in order, riven with rivalries and hatreds, are we to venture out into space? By the time we are ready

157

to settle even the nearest of planetary systems, we will have changed. The simple passage of so many generations will have changed us. Necessity will have changed us. We are an adaptable species. It will not be we who reach Alpha Centauri and the other nearby stars. It will be a species very much like us. But with more of our strengths and fewer of our weaknesses. More confident, far-seeing, capable and prudent. For all of our failings, despite our limitations and fallibilities, we humans are capable of greatness."

– Carl Sagan, The Pale Blue Dot

Not so long ago, we were nomads, living off what we could hunt and pick up on our way. We were humans, yes, but for hundreds of thousand of years, we lived very differently from how we live today. We lived in small tribes, subject to the elements of nature, striving to survive. Then something changed us. First the agricultural, then the industrial revolution, coupled with the discovery of cheap and abundant energy, lead us to an era of scientific discovery, exploration, and seemingly boundless growth. This has brought us all the modern comforts that we now take for granted. The computer or the book you are holding to read this very sentence, the artificial light in the room you are using to see the pages, the heating or air conditioning system to keep you comfortable, the electricity that runs your house; all this could not have been possible without the convergence of human ingenuity, technology, energy, and an economic system to drive them all.

Take the US as an example. Plotting the data from the Energy Information Agency on US energy use since 1650 we see a remarkably smooth trajectory in the energy consumption curve, steady at almost 3% per year.

In Figure B.1 you can see total US energy consumption in all forms since 1650. The vertical scale is logarithmic, so that an exponential curve resulting from a constant growth rate appears as a straight line. The red line corresponds to an annual growth rate of 2.9%.[234]

Now let us perform a thought experiment. Assuming we continue on this trajectory, how far can we go, trying to catch the 'Road Runner of infinite energy', until we realise there is nothing below us, and that we will eventually fall down the cliff like Wile E. Coyote? To make things easier, let us take the conservative estimate of 2.3% growth per year, instead of the 3% we have experienced in reality. This fits nicely with our Fermi guesstimate of the thought experiment, because every 100 years we have a factor of 10 increase[235], which simply means that after a century we multiply by ten the amount from where we started.

Today we use globally an average of 15 terawatts (tw) of power. Being 7 billion of us, that means that we *should* consume a little over 2 kilowatts (kw) per capita. The US and Canada use about 10 kw per capita, or almost five times what

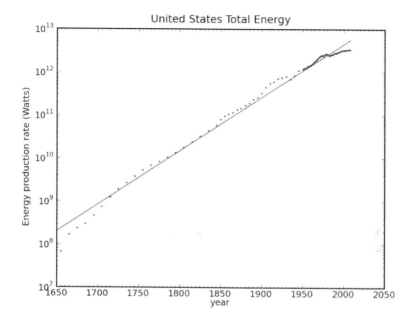

Figure B.1: Total US Energy consumption in all forms since 1650. Data source: EIA. Image Courtesy of prof. Tom Murphy.

they should, if we wanted to distribute the pie fairly among nations. In contrast Europeans, although they have a standard of living similar to North Americans, can manage pretty well with only half of that (Italy uses 3.6 kw, the U.K. Is at 4.2). Mexico is right in the middle at 2 kw, and at the opposite end of the spectrum, in Bangladesh, people use a mere 0.2 kw pro capita, on average.[236] Now imagine we cover *all the Earth's land surface* with high efficiency solar panels (operating at 20%), we can extract 7,000 tw of power, or about 470 times our current use. Remember that at 2.3% growth we get a factor of 10 every 100 years, so 15 tw quickly becomes 150. If we wait for another 100 years we get 1500 tw. In 300 years we have reached 15,000 tw, more than double the amount of energy gathered by a planet's worth of solar energy. Take a step back and we see that in a mere 270 years following this path, all the Earth's surface covered with solar panels will not be enough to provide for our hungry needs. 270 years might seem like a long time, but in terms of civilisation's history is just the blink of an eye.

But why am I so pessimistic? Surely by that time we will have exceeded the 20% efficiency of solar panels. New minds, new technology, infinite possibilities! OK, let?s laugh in the face of thermodynamics (that bitch!), we will operate at 100% efficiency. That only buys us a factor of five, or about 70 years. Remember that we just covered all the Earth land area (who needs food anyway?), so why stop there? We have the oceans, too. Let us make a gigantic array of solar photovoltaics, as big as entire surface of the Earth, operating at the impossible efficiency of 100%. Never mind the fact that virtually all life would be destroyed (including us), we need more energy! This helps (the imaginary) us for another 55 years at most. To sum up, in about 400 years of growth we used up *all* the available energy on Earth coming from the Sun.

But, you might object, we have other energies! Need I remind you that biomass, wind, and hydroelectricity all derive from the sun's radiation? What about fossil fuels? First off, we know that they are going to disappear pretty quickly, and that they will be depleted before the end of the century. Secondly, fossil fuels come from the Sun, too. They are dead plants that over millions of years became concentrated forms of hydrocarbon energy. As of today, we have only three energy sources that do not come from sunlight: nuclear, geothermal, and tidal processes (which are derived from the Moon's gravitation pull), the latter two of which are inconsequential for this analysis, at a few terawatts apiece.

At this point, I know you Star Trek fans will be outraged by my simple-mindedness and lack of vision. Why confine ourselves to the Earth? Clearly the future is in space. Why don't we build a Dyson sphere and surround the entire Sun with solars panels? And while we are at it, let us make them ultra thin (4 mm thick), with perfect 100% efficiency. Never mind the fact that we would need to the use an Earth's worth of materials. At 2.3% growth rate, we only get 1,300 years of energy.

Obviously I'm not making any sense, why would we want to use up the very source of life of this planet? Let the Sun be, and use *other* stars, we have a whole galaxy as our backyard! 100 billion stars, all waiting to be sucked up by our energy 'black hole'. Never mind the small problem of circumventing the speed of light (we will have cracked it by that time), let us assume that interstellar travel is doable. Recall that each factor of ten takes us 100 years down the road. One-hundred billion is eleven factors of ten, so the milky way only gives us 1,100 additional years. Exponential growth. In about 2,500 years from now, we would be using a large galaxy's worth of energy. That is, assuming we can achieve perfect efficiency (impossible?), circumvent the limitations of the speed of light (highly improbable), and that the energy utilised to gather and transport that of another star is less than what we get out of it (I would not bet on it).

Suppose we overcome those 'minor' engineering issues. Surely by that time we will have negative energy ships that fold space-time, we will have mastered quantum mechanics and its mysterious tunnelling effects; nuclear fusion will be a piece of cake! And that can provide infinite energy and abundance forever, right? Well, to put it simply, no. *No matter what the technology*, a sustained 2.3%

energy growth rate would require us to produce as much energy as the entire sun within 400 years. Even if we build a nuclear fusion power plant, it is going to run a little warm. Thermodynamics requires that if we generated sun-comparable power on Earth, the surface of the Earth – being smaller than that of the sun – would have to be hotter than the surface of the Sun![237]

These results are obviously ludicrous. It is clear that we are not going to boil ourselves alive, and we will not make the planet completely inhospitable for our species. From a purely mathematical and physical perspective, we know one thing: we are not going to continue to grow at an exponential rate of energy consumption. It is simply impossible. No matter the technology, no matter how inventive and smart we become, no matter the energy source, thermodynamics would not allow it. That means that if we still buy into the growth paradigm, it should be based on some sort of growth that does not require either physical (goods) or energetic resources. What does that mean? The only way to keep growing without breaking the laws of physics, is to produce only intangible goods and services.

Let?s all be musicians, writers, psychologists, massage therapists! And let?s all sell each other every conceivable moment of our lives! Not only our knowledge and expertise, but also our intellectual and creative capabilities, our ideas, and, why not, our intimacy! And always at a higher price. We will be living in virtual worlds, like Second Life, or an evolution of Facebook and Twitter. And we will spend our time selling each other digital goods with digital currencies. We have already begun the gamification in many aspects of our lives, why not take it the next level? Everything is going to be a big, big game. What a bright future awaits us

Sounds absurd? Yes, I agree. But it is the only way you can keep this growth business up, without crashing into something that is not just absurd but also plain impossible.

It is quite striking that these results are as uncontroversial as they are ignored by mainstream economists. I could not find a single economist who would debate the physicists and the mathematicians about the accuracy of this analysis. They simply choose to ignore it. But for how long can we continue to play this game of "don't see, don't hear, don't tell"? Even people like Ray Kurzweil, who have a remarkable understanding of what exponential growth means and how it affects the global economy, do not seem to be bothered in the least by these results. Do not get me wrong, Ray is a pretty smart guy, so if he is not concerned maybe I am missing something. But I talked to economists and futurists, read their books, and still did not find a solution to this conundrum. According to them, the economy will find a way, because…well because it *always finds a way*. This sort of tautology would be understandable if it was supported by some evidence other than the past growth on this planet, which never approached the physical limits of what is actually feasible.

One of the few criticisms I have heard against the impossibility of continuous growth is that I was not considering the most important aspect of the market system: *efficiency*. The argument goes as follows. As technology progresses efficiency increases, therefore there is no reason to worry, and the market self-adjusts. I want you to understand why people who make this claim are either wrong and unaware of it, or they are simply lying. Giving the benefit of the doubt, I would argue that in most cases they are very sincere. They just have no idea what they are talking about.

Let us see the how the efficiency argument plays out. One thing to understand is that regardless of the technology you use, regardless of how smart you are, or how good you are as an entrepreneur, there are physical limits to the efficiency gains you can achieve. No matter how hard you try, you cannot exceed the efficiency of 100%. Actually, thermodynamics does not even allow you to reach 100% efficiency, but we can get close enough for any practical purposes. Fossil-fuel and nuclear power plants operate at 30-40% efficiency, and automobiles operate at 15-25% efficiency. Heat engines therefore account for about two-thirds of the total energy use in the US (27% in transportation, 36% in electricity production, a bit in industry). Professor of Physics Tom Murphy, who originally made this analysis, continues:

> "The efficiency of gasoline-powered cars cannot easily improve by any large factor, but the effective efficiency can be improved significantly by transitioning to electric drive trains. While a car getting 40 m.p.g. may have a 20% efficient gasoline engine, a battery-powered drive train might achieve something like 70% efficiency (85% efficiency in charging batteries, 85% in driving the electric motor). The factor of 3.5 improvement in efficiency suggests effective mileage performance of 140 m.p.g. One caution, however: if the input electricity comes from a fossil-fuel power plant operating at 40% efficiency and 90% transmission efficiency, the effective fossil-to-locomotion efficiency is reduced to 25%, and is not such a significant step. [...]
> Given that two-thirds of our energy resource is burned in heat engines, and that these cannot improve much more than a factor of two, more significant gains elsewhere are diminished in value. For instance, replacing the 10% of our energy budget spent on direct heat (e.g., in furnaces and hot water heaters) with heat pumps operating at their maximum theoretical efficiency effectively replaces a 10% expenditure with a 1% expenditure. A factor of ten sounds like a fantastic improvement, but the overall efficiency improvement in

society is only 9%. Likewise with light bulb replacement: large gains in a small sector. We should still pursue these efficiency improvements with vigour, but we should not expect this gift to provide a form of unlimited growth."[238]

To sum up, the most we might expect to achieve is to double net efficiency increase, before theoretical limits and engineering realities clamp down. At the present 1% overall rate, this means we might expect to run out of gain this century. So much for the efficiency argument.

You must forgive me if I stress this point to the point of exhaustion, but I feel compelled to repeat and emphasise what I wrote earlier: what we described is irrespective of the technology, the time, or the market. This is physics. No matter what we do, with a 2.3% growth per year (which is much lower than the rate of the last 150 years), we hit the physical limits in a few decades at best. Not exactly a plan for long term survival, is it? Without projecting too much into the future, practical limits to efficiency will affect most of us within our lifetime, and most certainly that of our children's. This is no laughing matter. Next time you hear somebody claiming that economic growth can continue forever, and that you just do not get it because you are not taking efficiency into account, you know what to respond.

To conclude, I would like to take and look at it from a larger perspective. As Prof. Murphy pointed out, we, as a society, are like children asking their parents for a pony. We have not learned to take care of our gerbil (peak oil, environmental degradation), yet we are asking for a pony (fusion or whatever supposedly infinite supply of energy we have in mind, space colonisation, infinite growth). This is quite arrogant and irresponsible at the same time.

We ought to be better than spoiled little children. It is time to grow up and move forward.

Last thank you note

As promised, a last thank you note to some remarkable individuals who supported me during the IndieGoGo crowdfunding campaign: Maurizio Bisogni, Susi Guarise, Simone Roda, Alessandro Ronca, Sirio Marchi, Lorenzo Grespan, Søren Lassen Schmidt, Steve Friedrich, and Jason Souders.

Thank you again.

Notes

ACKNOWLEDGEMENTS

1.   I should say AFK. I believe the Internet is real.

CHAPTER 1 – UNEMPLOYMENT TODAY

2.   *US Posts Stronger Solid Growth in July*, Mokoto Rich, 2011. The New York Times.
     `http://www.nytimes.com/2011/08/06/business/economy/us-posts`
     `-solid-job-gains-amid-fears.html?pagewanted=all`

3.   *Private Sector Up, Government Down*, David Leonhardt, 2011. The New York Times.
     `http://economix.blogs.nytimes.com/2011/08/05/private-sector`
     `-up-government-down/`

4.   *Jobs Deficit, Investment Deficit, Fiscal Deficit*, Laura D'Andrea Tyson, 2011. The New York Times.
     `http://economix.blogs.nytimes.com/2011/07/29/jobs-deficit`
     `-investment-deficit-fiscal-deficit/`

5.   *The Employment Situation*, 2012. Bureau Of Labor Statistics
     `http://www.bls.gov/news.release/pdf/empsit.pdf`

6.   *Civilian Labor Force Participation Rate.* Bureau of Labor Statistics.
     `http://data.bls.gov/timeseries/LNS11300000`

7.   *Race Against The Machine: How the Digital Revolution is Accelerating Innovation, Driving Productivity, and Irreversibly Transforming Employment and the Economy*, Erik Brynjolfsson and Andrew McAfee, 2011. Digital Frontier Press.
     `http://raceagainstthemachine.com`

8.   *The End of Work Website*, Jeremy Rifkin.
     `http://www.foet.org/books/end-work.html`

9. *The End of Work*, Wikipedia.
   http://en.wikipedia.org/wiki/The_End_of_Work

10. *A rough 10 years for the middle class*, Annalyn Censky, 2011. CNNMoney.
    http://money.cnn.com/2011/09/21/news/economy/middle_class
    _income/index.htm.

11. *22 Statistics That Prove That The Middle Class Is Being Systematically Wiped Out Of Existence In America*, Michael Snyder, 2010. Business Insider.
    http://www.businessinsider.com/22-statistics-that-prove
    -the-middle-class-is-being-systematically-wiped-out-of
    -existence-in-america-2010-7

12. *US Congressional Budget Office*, 2011. Graphics adapted from Mother Jones.
    http://motherjones.com/politics/2011/02/income-inequality
    -in-america-chart-graph

13. *Building a Better America – One Wealth Quintile at a Time*, Michael I. Norton, Dan Ariely. Journal Perspectives on Psychological Science.
    http://pps.sagepub.com/content/6/1/9

14. I highly recommend the four-part video series *Everything is a Remix* by Kirby Ferguson, one of the best piece of work I have ever seen on this subject.
    http://www.everythingisaremix.info

CHAPTER 2 – THE LUDDITE FALLACY

15. *The Skilled Labourer 1760-1832*, Hammond, J.L.; Hammond, Barbara, 1919. London: Longmans, Green and co.; p. 259.
    http://www.archive.org/details/skilledlabourer00hammiala

16. *Difference Engine: Luddite legacy*, 2011. The Economist.
    http://www.economist.com/blogs/babbage/2011/11/artificial
    -intelligence

17. *Productivity and unemployment*, 2003. Marginal Revolution.
    http://www.marginalrevolution.com/marginalrevolution/2003/
    12/productivity_an.html

18. *Harmonised unemployment rate by gender*. Eurostat.
    http://epp.eurostat.ec.europa.eu/tgm/table.do?tab=table
    &language=en&pcode=teilm020&tableSelection=1&plugin=1

19. *American Notes: Vonnegut's Gospel*, 1970. Time Magazine.
    http://www.time.com/time/magazine/article/
    0,9171,878826,00.html

CHAPTER 3 – EXPONENTIAL GROWTH

20. *Sustainability 101: Arithmetic, Population, and Energy*, Albert Bartlett.
http://jclahr.com/bartlett/

21. The reason is for this quite simple. 70 is approximately $100ln(2)$. So, $doublingtime = 100ln(2) = 69.3$. If you want the time to triple the formula is: $triplingtime = 100ln(3) = 109.8$. The time to grow n-times is $100ln(n)$.

22. *Rule of 70*. Wikipedia.
http://en.wikipedia.org/wiki/Rule_of_70

23. According to other accounts, it was a legendary Dravida Vellalar*Dravidian peoples* is a term used to refer to the diverse groups of people who natively speak languages belonging to the Dravidian language family. Populations of speakers of around 220 million are found mostly in Southern India. *Vellalars* (also, Velalars, Vellalas) were, originally, an elite caste of Tamil agricultural landlords in Tamil Nadu, Kerala states in India and in neighbouring Sri Lanka; they were the nobility, aristocracy of the ancient Tamil order (Chera/Chola/Pandya/Sangam era) and had close relations with the different royal dynasties named Sessa or Sissa.
http://en.wikipedia.org/wiki/Dravidian_peoples
http://en.wikipedia.org/wiki/Vellalar There exist many different variation of the same story, one set in the Roman Empire involving a brave general and his Cæsar, another with two merchants at the market, all different situations producing the same result.
http://en.wikipedia.org/wiki/Wheat_and_chessboard_problem

24. Image courtesy of Wikipedia.
http://en.wikipedia.org/wiki/File:Wheat_Chessboard_with_line.svg

CHAPTER 4 – INFORMATION TECHNOLOGY

25. *Cramming more components onto integrated circuits*, Gordon E. Moore, 1965. Electronics Magazine. p. 4.
http://download.intel.com/museum/Moores_Law/Articles-Press_Releases/Gordon_Moore_1965_Article.pdf

26. *The Law of Accelerating Returns March 7*, Ray Kurzweil, 2001.
http://www.kurzweilai.net/the-law-of-accelerating-returns

CHAPTER 5 – INTELLIGENCE

27. The Chinese room is a thought experiment presented by John Searle. It supposes that there is a program that gives a computer the ability to carry on an intelligent conversation in written Chinese. If the program is given to someone who speaks only English to execute the instructions of the program by hand, then in theory, the English speaker would also be able to carry on a conversation in written Chinese. However, the English speaker would not be able to understand the conversation. Similarly, Searle concludes, a computer executing the program would not understand the conversation either.
    http://plato.stanford.edu/entries/chinese-room/
    http://en.wikipedia.org/wiki/Chinese_room

28. A 'facepalm' is the physical gesture of placing one's hand flat across one's face or lowering one's face into one's hand or hands. The gesture is found in many cultures as a display of frustration, disappointment, embarrassment, shock or surprise. It has been popularised as an Internet meme based on an image of the character Captain Jean-Luc Picard performing the gesture in a *Star Trek: The Next Generation* episode "DéjàQ".
    http://picardfacepalm.com/
    http://en.wikipedia.org/wiki/Facepalm

29. *Intelligence Without Reason*, Rodney A. Brooks, 1991. Massachusetts Institute Of Technology Artificial Intelligence Laboratory.
    http://people.csail.mit.edu/brooks/papers/AIM-1293.pdf

30. *On Intelligence: How a New Understanding of the Brain will Lead to the Creation of Truly Intelligent Machines*, Jeff Hawkins, 2004; *The Emotion Machine: Commonsense Thinking, Artificial Intelligence , and the Future of the Human Mind*, Marvin Minsky, 2006

CHAPTER 6 – ARTIFICIAL INTELLIGENCE

31. The example is taken from *The Lights in the Tunnel: Automation, Accelerating Technology and the Economy of the Future*, Martin Ford, 2009. CreateSpace. pp.64-67.

32. "In reality, there is another factor that might slow the adoption of full automation in Radiology: that is malpractice liability. Because the result of a mistake or oversight in reading a medical scan would likely be dire for the patient, the maker of a completely automated system would assume huge potential liability in the event of errors. This liability, of course, also exists

for radiologists, but it is distributed across thousands of doctors. However, it is certainly possible that legislation and/or court decisions will largely remove this barrier in the future. For example, in February 2008, the U.S. Supreme Court ruled in an 8-1 decision that, in certain cases, medical device manufacturers are protected from product liability cases as long as the FDA has approved the device. In general, we can expect that non-technological factors such as product liability or the power of organised labor will slow automation in certain fields, but the overall trend will remain relentless" from: *The Lights in the Tunnel: Automation, Accelerating Technology and the Economy of the Future*, Martin Ford, 2009. CreateSpace. p.67.

33. *Can AI Fight Terrorism?*, Juval Aviv, 2009. Forbes.
    `http://www.forbes.com/2009/06/18/ai-terrorism-interfor`
    `-opinions-contributors-artificial-intelligence-09-juval`
    `-aviv.html`

34. *Smart CCTV System Would Use Algorithm to Zero in on Crime-Like Behavior*, Clay Dillow, 2011. Popular Science.
    `http://www.popsci.com/technology/article/2011-08/new-cctv`
    `-system-would-use-behavior-recognition-zero-crimes`

35. *The offshoring of radiology: myths and realities*, Martin Stack, Myles Gartland, Timothy Keane, 2007. SAM Advanced Management Journal.
    `http://www.accessmylibrary.com/coms2/summary`
    `_028630757731_ITM`

36. *Comparing machines and humans on a visual categorization test*, François Fleuret, Ting Li, Charles Dubout, Emma K. Wampler, Steven Yantis, and Donald Geman, 2011. Proceedings of the National Academy of Sciences.
    `http://www.pnas.org/content/early/2011/10/11/`
    `1109168108.full.pdf`

37. *The Singularity Is Near: When Humans Transcend Biology*, Kurzweil, 2005. Penguin Books.

CHAPTER 7 – EVIDENCE OF AUTOMATION

38. According to the Japan Vending Machine Manufactures Association website, there are 8,610,521 vending machines in Japan, or one machine for every 14 people.
    `http://www.jvma.or.jp/information/qa_01.html`

39. *Amazon buys army of robots*, Julianne Pepitone, 2012. CNN Money.
    `http://money.cnn.com/2012/03/20/technology/amazon-kiva`
    `-robots/index.htm?hpt=hp_t3`

40. Tesco Homeplus Virtual Subway Store in South Korea.
     `http://www.youtube.com/watch?v=fGaVFRzTTP4`

41. The Weight of Walmart (Infographic)
     `http://frugaldad.com/2011/12/01/weight-of-walmart`
     `-infographic/`

42. *Strikes End at Two Chinese Automotive Suppliers*, 2010. Reuters.
     `http://www.reuters.com/article/idUSTRE66L0A220100722`

43. *Table 3. The Circuits Assembly Top 50 EMS Companies*, 2009. Circuits
     Assembly.
     `http://circuitsassembly.com/cms/images/stories/ArticleImages/`
     `1003/1003buetow_table3.pdf`

44. *Forbes Global 2000: The World's Biggest Companies – Hon Hai Precision
     Industry*, 2010. Forbes.
     `http://www.forbes.com/companies/hon-hai-precision/`

45. *Which is the world's biggest employer?*, 2012. BBC News.
     `http://www.bbc.co.uk/news/magazine-17429786`

46. *Apple partnership boosting Foxconn market share*, 2010. CNET.
     `http://news.cnet.com/8301-13579_3-20011800-37.html`

47. *Foxconn to replace workers with 1 million robots in 3 years*, July 2011.
     Xinhuanet News.
     `http://news.xinhuanet.com/english2010/china/2011-07/30/c`
     `_131018764.htm`

48. *Companies Making The Necessary Transition From Industrial To Service
     Robots*, 2012. Singularity Hub.
     `http://singularityhub.com/2012/06/06/companies-making-the`
     `-necessary-transition-from-industrial-to-service-robots/`

49. emphFoxconn Factories Are Labour Camps: Report. South China Morning
     Post.

50. *Foxconn Security Guards Caught Beating Factory Workers*, 2010. Shang-
     haiist.
     `http://shanghaiist.com/2010/05/20/foxconn-security-guards`
     `-beating.php`

51. *Revealed: Inside the Chinese Suicide Sweatshop Where Workers Toil in
     34-Hour Shifts To Make Your iPod*, 2010. Daily Mail (London).
     `http://www.dailymail.co.uk/news/article-1285980/Revealed`
     `-Inside-Chinese-suicide-sweatshop-workers-toil-34-hour`
     `-shifts-make-iPod.html`

52. *Suicides at Foxconn*, 2010. The Economist.
    http://www.economist.com/node/16231588

53. *Canon Camera Factory To Go Fully Automated, Phase Out Human Workers*, June 2012. Singularity Hub.
    http://singularityhub.com/2012/06/06/canon-camera-factory-to-go-fully-automated-phase-out-human-workers/

54. *China Is Replacing Its Workers With Robots*, 2012. Business Insider.
    http://www.businessinsider.com/credit-suisse-chinese-automation-boom-2012-8

55. *The Machines Are Taking Over*, Sep. 14, 2012. The New York Times
    http://www.nytimes.com/2012/09/16/magazine/how-computerized-tutors-are-learning-to-teach-humans.html

56. *Why Software Is Eating The World*, 2011. The Wall Street Journal.
    http://on.wsj.com/pC7IrX

57. In the TV series Star Trek, a replicator works by rearranging subatomic particles, which are abundant everywhere in the universe, to form molecules and arrange those molecules to form the object. For example, to create a pork chop, the replicator would first form atoms of carbon, hydrogen, nitrogen, etc., then arrange them into amino acids, proteins, and cells, and assemble the particles into the form of a pork chop.
    http://en.wikipedia.org/wiki/Replicator_(Star_Trek)

58. *Will 3D Printing Change The World?*, 2012. Forbes.
    http://www.forbes.com/sites/gcaptain/2012/03/06/will-3d-printing-change-the-world/print/

59. Objet Connex 3D printers.
    http://www.ops-uk.com/3d-printers/objet-connex

60. *iPhone 4's Retina Display Explained*, Chris Brandrick, 2010. PC World.
    http://www.pcworld.com/article/198201/iphone_4s_retina_display_explained.html

61. 3D printing.
    http://www.explainingthefuture.com/3dprinting.html

62. *A primer on 3D printing*, Lisa Harouni, 2001. TEDSalon London Spring 2011.
    http://www.ted.com/talks/lisa_harouni_a_primer_on_3d_printing.html

63. *3D-printed prosthetics offer amputees new lease on life*, 2012. Reuters.
    http://www.reuters.com/video/2012/02/27/3d-printed-prosthetics-offer-amputees-ne?videoId=230878689

64. *3D printer used to make bone-like material*, 2011. Washington State University.
    http://wsutoday.wsu.edu/pages/publications.asp
    ?Action=Detail&PublicationID=29002&TypeID=1

65. *Making a bit of me, a machine that prints organs is coming to market*, 2010. The Economist.
    http://www.economist.com/node/15543683

66. *Transplant jaw made by 3D printer claimed as first*, 2012. BBC News.
    http://www.bbc.com/news/technology-16907104

67. *What drives us*. Bespoke.
    http://www.bespokeinnovations.com/content/what-drives-us

68. Thingiverse.
    http://www.thingiverse.com

69. *First Downloaded and 3D Printed Pirate Bay Ship Arrives*, 2012. Torrent-Freak.
    http://torrentfreak.com/first-downloaded-and-3d-printed
    -pirate-bay-ship-arrives-120205/

70. *30-storey building built in 15 days Construction time lapse*. YouTube.
    http://www.youtube.com/watch?&v=Hdpf-MQM9vY

71. *Time lapse captures 30-story hotel construction that took just 15 days to build*, 2012. The Blaze.
    http://www.theblaze.com/stories/time-lapse-captures
    -30-story-hotel-construction-that-took-just-15-days-to
    -build/

72. *Annenberg Foundation Puts Robotic Disaster Rebuilding Technology on Fast Track*, 2005. University of Southern California School of Engineering.
    http://viterbi.usc.edu/news/news/2005/news_20051110.htm

73. *House-Bot*, December 30, 2005. The Science Channel.

74. *Census of Fatal Occupational Injuries Summary*, 2010. Bureau of Labour Statistics.
    http://bls.gov/news.release/cfoi.nr0.htm

75. *Caterpillar Inc. Funds Viterbi 'Print-a-House' Construction Technology*, 2008. University of Southern California School of Engineering.
    http://viterbi.usc.edu/news/news/2008/caterpillar-inc-funds
    .htm

76. *Colloquium with Behrokh Khoshnevis*, 2009. Massachusetts Institute of Technology.
    http://www.media.mit.edu/node/2277

77. *GSP-09 Team Project: ACASA*, 2009. YouTube.
    http://www.youtube.com/watch?v=172Wne1t_2Q

78. Problem?
    http://www.urbandictionary.com/define.php?term=trolling

79. *Are Sportswriters Really Necessary? Narrative Science's software takes sports stats and spits out articles*, Justin Bachman, 2010. Newsweek.
    http://www.businessweek.com/magazine/content/10_19/b
    4177037188386.htm

80. *Garry Kasparov vs. Deep Blue*, Frederic Friedel. Daily Chess Columns.
    http://www.chessbase.com/columns/column.asp?pid=146

81. In computer science, brute-force search or exhaustive search, also known as "generate and test??, is a simple but very general problem-solving technique that consists of systematically enumerating all possible candidates for the solution and checking whether each candidate satisfies the problem's stated goal. For example, a brute-force algorithm to find the divisors of a natural number n is to enumerate all integers from 1 to the square-root of n, and check whether each of them divides n without remainder.
    http://en.wikipedia.org/wiki/Brute-force_search

82. *Chatbots fail to convince judges that they're human*, 2011. New Scientist.
    http://www.newscientist.com/blogs/onepercent/2011/10/turing
    -test-chatbots-kneel-bef.html

83. *Did you Know?*, Jeopardy!
    http://www.jeopardy.com/showguide/abouttheshow/showhistory/

84. *Computer Program to Take On 'Jeopardy!'*, John Markoff, 2009. The New York Times.
    http://www.nytimes.com/2009/04/27/technology/27jeopardy
    .html

85. According to IBM, Watson is a workload optimised system designed for complex analytics, made possible by integrating massively parallel POWER7 processors and the IBM DeepQA software to answer Jeopardy! questions in under three seconds. Watson is made up of a cluster of ninety IBM Power 750 servers (plus additional I/O, network and cluster controller nodes in 10 racks) with a total of 2880 POWER7 processor cores and 16 Terabytes of RAM. Each Power 750 server uses a 3.5 GHz POWER7 eight-core processor, with four threads per core. The POWER7 processor's massively parallel processing capability is an ideal match for Watson's IBM DeepQA software which is embarrassingly parallel (that is a workload that is easily split up into multiple parallel tasks).
    http://www-03.ibm.com/systems/power/advantages/watson/index
    .html

86. *Instant Reaction: Man-Made Minds*, David Ferrucci, 2011. World SCience Festival.
    `http://worldsciencefestival.com/blog/instant_reaction_man`
    `_made_minds`

87. *IBM's Watson heads to medical school*, Nick Wakeman, 2011. Washington Technology.
    `http://washingtontechnology.com/articles/2011/02/17/ibm`
    `-watson-next-steps.aspx`
    Wikipedia, Watson.
    `https://en.wikipedia.org/wiki/Watson_%28computer`

88. *Mission Control, Built for Cities. I.B.M. Takes 'Smarter Cities' Concept to Rio de Janeiro*, Natasha Singer, 2012. New York Times.
    `http://www.nytimes.com/2012/03/04/business/ibm-takes`
    `-smarter-cities-concept-to-rio-de-janeiro.html`
    `?pagewanted=all`

89. *Will IBM Watson Be Your Next Mayor?*, 2012. Slashdot.
    `http://yro.slashdot.org/story/12/04/27/0029256/will-ibm`
    `-watson-be-your-next-mayor`

90. *Computers to Acquire Control of the Physical World*, P. Magrassi, A. Panarella, N. Deighton, G. Johnson, 2001. Gartner research report. T-14-0301.

91. *A World of Smart Objects*, P. Magrassi, T. Berg, 2002. Gartner research report. R-17-2243.
    `http://www.gartner.com/DisplayDocument?id=366151`

92. *The Internet of Things*. Wikipedia.
    `http://en.wikipedia.org/wiki/Internet_of_Things`

93. *Study: Intelligent Cars Could Boost Highway Capacity by 273%*, 2012. Institute of Electrical and Electronics Engineers.
    `http://spectrum.ieee.org/automaton/robotics/artificial`
    `-intelligence/intelligent-cars-could-boost-highway`
    `-capacity-by-273`

CHAPTER 8 – SOCIAL ACCEPTANCE

94. *INTERNET USAGE STATISTICS. The Internet Big Picture.* World Internet Users and Population Stats.
    `http://www.internetworldstats.com/stats.htm`

95. *Freedom on the Net 2011 – A Global Assessment of Internet and Digital Media Freedom*, 2011. Freedom House.
http://www.freedomhouse.org/report/freedom-net/freedom-net-2011

96. Internet censorship in the United States. Wikipedia.
http://en.wikipedia.org/wiki/Internet_censorship_in_the_United_States

97. *PROTECT IP / SOPA Breaks The Internet*, Kirby Ferguson, 2012.
http://vimeo.com/31100268

98. Stop Online Piracy Act. Wikipedia.
http://en.wikipedia.org/wiki/Stop_Online_Piracy_Act

99. *Anti-Counterfeiting Trade Agreement What is ACTA?*. Electronic Frontier Foundation.
https://www.eff.org/issues/acta

100. Extracts from the Slashdot discussion on SOPA, 2012. Slashdot.
http://tech.slashdot.org/story/11/12/16/1943257/congresss-techno-ignorance-no-longer-funny

101. *The Top 0.1% Of The Nation Earn Half Of All Capital Gains*, Robert Lenzner, 2011. Forbes.
http://www.forbes.com/sites/robertlenzner/2011/11/20/the-top-0-1-of-the-nation-earn-half-of-all-capital-gains/

102. *A nationally representative and continuing assessment of English language literary skills of American Adults*, National Assessment of Adult Literacy (NAAL). National Center for Education Statistics.
http://nces.ed.gov/naal/kf_demographics.asp

103. *Human Development Report 2009: Overcoming barriers: Human mobility and development*, 2009. United Nations Development Programme.
http://hdr.undp.org/en/media/HDR_2009_EN_Complete.pdf

104. *Americans' Global Warming Concerns Continue to Drop*, 2010. Gallup.
http://www.gallup.com/poll/126560/americans-global-warming-concerns-continue-drop.aspx

105. *Climate scepticism 'on the rise', BBC poll shows*, 2010. BBC.
http://news.bbc.co.uk/2/hi/8500443.stm

106. *Climate change: How do we know?*. NASA.
http://climate.nasa.gov/evidence/

107. *Climate Change Skeptic Results Released Today*, 2011. Slashdot.
http://news.slashdot.org/story/11/10/31/1255205/climate-change-skeptic-results-released-today

108. *Robotic Nation*, Marshall Brain.
http://marshallbrain.com/robotic-nation.htm

CHAPTER 9 – UNEMPLOYMENT TOMORROW

109. *Employed persons by detailed occupation, sex, race, and Hispanic or Latino ethnicity.* Bureau of Labor Statistics.
`ftp://ftp.bls.gov/pub/special.requests/lf/aat11.txt`

110. *Employment Situation Summary.* Bureau of Labor Statistics.
`http://www.bls.gov/news.release/empsit.nr0.htm`

111. *Employment status of the civilian noninstitutional population, 1940 to date.* Bureau of Labor Statistics.
`ftp://ftp.bls.gov/pub/special.requests/lf/aat1.txt`

112. *Eurozone Unemployment Hits 10.9%, A Record High,* 2012. Huffington post.
`http://www.huffingtonpost.com/2012/05/02/eurozone-unemployment-hits-record-high_n_1470237.html`

113. *The 86 million invisible unemployed,* Annalyn Censky, 2012. CNNMoney.
`http://money.cnn.com/2012/05/03/news/economy/unemployment-rate/index.htm`

114. *Ken Robinson says schools kill creativity.* Ken Robinson, 2006. TED Global.
`http://www.ted.com/talks/ken_robinson_says_schools_kill_creativity.html`

115. *Sir Ken Robinson: Bring on the learning revolution!,* Ken Robinson, 2010. TED Global.
`http://www.ted.com/talks/sir_ken_robinson_bring_on_the_revolution.html`

116. I obviously do not think people are "excess baggage", quite the opposite. But in the eyes of a multinational corporation inefficient workers mean loss of profit, and this is what they ultimately mean to them. There are very few enlightened companies that value people over profits.

117. *Facebook faces EU curbs on selling users' interests to advertisers,* Jason Lewis, 2011. The Telegraph.
`http://www.telegraph.co.uk/technology/facebook/8917836/Facebook-faces-EU-curbs-on-selling-users-interests-to-advertisers.html`

118. *Does Facebook sell my information?.* Facebook.
`https://www.facebook.com/help/?faq=152637448140583`

119. Albert Einstein quotes. ThinkExist.
`http://thinkexist.com/quotation/if_you_can-t_explain_it_simply-you_don-t/186838.html`

120. Neuroplasticity refers to the susceptibility to physiological changes of the nervous system, due to changes in behaviour, environment, neural processes, or parts of the body other than the nervous system. It occurs on a variety of levels, ranging from cellular changes due to learning, to large-scale changes involved in cortical remapping in response to injury. The role of neuroplasticity is widely recognised in healthy development, learning, memory, and recovery from brain damage. Recent findings are revealing that many aspects of the brain remain plastic even into adulthood.

References:

- Pascual-Leone, A., Freitas, C., Oberman, L., Horvath, J. C., Halko, M., Eldaief, M. et al. (2011). *Characterizing brain cortical plasticity and network dynamics across the age-span in health and disease with TMS-EEG and TMS-fMRI.* Brain Topography, 24, 302-315.

- Pascual-Leone, A., Amedi, A., Fregni, F., & Merabet, L. B. (2005). *The plastic human brain cortex.* Annual Review of Neuroscience, 28, 377-401.

- Rakic, P. (January 2002). *Neurogenesis in adult primate neocortex: an evaluation of the evidence.* Nature Reviews Neuroscience.

CHAPTER 10 – WORK IDENTITY

121. Cluster munitions are prohibited for those nations that ratify the Convention on Cluster Munitions, adopted in Dublin, Ireland in May 2008. The Convention entered into force and became binding international law upon ratifying states on 1 August, 2010, six months after being ratified by 30 states; as of August 2011, a total of 108 states had signed the Convention and 60 of those have ratified it. However, these type of bombs are still used extensively in wars and internal conflicts around the world. They are either produced and distributed by states that did not ratify this convention, or they find their way around through the black market. I could also have used another example, but I think you get the point.

122. *Corruption Perceptions Index 2010: In detail,* 2010. Transparency International.
http://www.transparency.org/policy_research/surveys_indices/cpi/2010/in_detail

123. *Intergenerational mobility in Europe and North America,* Blanden J., Gregg P., Machin S., 2005. London: Centre for Economic Performance, London School of Economics.

`http://cep.lse.ac.uk/about/news/IntergenerationalMobility`
`.pdf`

124. *The problems of relative deprivation: why some societies do better than others*, Richard Wilkinson, Kate Pickett, 2007. Social Science and Medicine 2007; 65. pp. 1965-78.
`http://www.equalitytrust.org.uk/docs/problems-of-relative`
`-deprivation.pdf`

CHAPTER 11 – THE PURSUIT OF HAPPINESS

125. *A Treatise of the Laws of Nature*, Richard Cumberland, 2005. Indianapolis: Liberty Fund. pp. 523-24.

126. *Essay Concerning Human Understanding, Book 2, Chapter 21, Section 51*, John Locke, 1690.

127. *Justifying America: The Declaration of Independence as a Rhetorical Document*, Stephen Lucas in Thomas W. Benson, ed., *American Rhetoric: Context and Criticism*, 1989.

128. *City of Ruins*, Chris Hedges, 2010. The Nation.
`http://www.thenation.com/article/155801/city-ruins`

129. *Remaining Awake Through a Great Revolution*, Martin Luther King Jr., 31 March 1968, sermon at the National Cathedral; published in *A Testament of Hope*, 1986

130. American Idol has consistently been the most popular show in the recent history of American television.
`http://en.wikipedia.org/wiki/List_of_most_watched`
`_television_broadcast`

131. Several acts of violence were reported on Black Friday over the course of the past few years.

   - *Wal-Mart worker dies in rush; two killed at toy store*, 2008. CNN.
     `http://edition.cnn.com/2008/US/11/28/black.friday`
     `.violence/index.html`

   - *Black Friday shopper arrested on weapons, drug charges in Boynton Beach | boynton, arrested, beach - Top Story - WPEC 12 West Palm Beach*, 2011. CBS.
     `http://www.cbs12.com/news/boynton-4729776-arrested`
     `-beach.html`

   - Black Friday – Violence. Wikipedia.
     `http://en.wikipedia.org/wiki/Black_Friday_(shopping`
     `)#Violence`

132. *The 1% are the very best destroyers of wealth the world has ever seen,* George Monbiot, 2011. The Guardian.
http://www.guardian.co.uk/commentisfree/2011/nov/07/one-per
-cent-wealth-destroyers.Emphasismine.

133. *How cognitive illusions blind us to reason,* Daniel Kahneman, 2011. The Guardian. http://www.guardian.co.uk/science/2011/oct/ 30/daniel-kahneman-cognitive-illusion-extract

134. *Disordered Personalities at Work,* Belinda Jane Board and Katarina Fritzon, 2005. Psychology, Crime & Law, Vol. 11(1). pp. 17-32.

135. *The network of global corporate control,* Stefania Vitali, James B. Glattfelder, and Stefano Battiston, 2011. ETH Zurich, Kreuzplatz 5, 8032 Zurich, Switzerland.
http://arxiv.org/PS_cache/arxiv/pdf/1107/1107.5728v2.pdf

CHAPTER 12 – THE SCORPION AND THE FROG

136. Adapted from an anonymous comment on Slashdot.
http://slashdot.org/comments.pl?sid=180945&cid=14970571

CHAPTER 13 – GROWTH AND HAPPINESS

137. *Quantitative Analysis of Culture Using Millions of Digitized Books,* Jean-Baptiste Michel, Yuan Kui Shen, Aviva Presser Aiden, Adrian Veres, Matthew K. Gray, William Brockman, The Google Books Team, Joseph P. Pickett, Dale Hoiberg, Dan Clancy, Peter Norvig, Jon Orwant, Steven Pinker, Martin A. Nowak, and Erez Lieberman Aiden, 2010. Science.
http://www.sciencemag.org/content/early/2010/12/15/science
.1199644

138. *Does Economic Growth Improve the Human Lot? Some Empirical Evidence,* Richard A. Easterlin, 1974. University of Pennsylvania.
http://graphics8.nytimes.com/images/2008/04/
16/business/Easterlin1974.pdf

139. *The happiness-income paradox revisited,* Richard A. Easterlin, Laura Angelescu McVey, Malgorzata Switek, Onnicha Sawangfa, and Jacqueline Smith Zweig, 2010. Proceedings of the National Academy of Sciences.
http://www.pnas.org/cgi/doi/10.1073/pnas.1015962107

140. *Money Doesn't Make People Happy,* 2006. Forbes.
http://www.forbes.com/2006/02/11/tim-harford-money_cz_th
_money06_0214harford.html

141. *Psychology 110 Lecture 20 – The Good Life: Happiness*, Prof. Paul Bloom. Yale University.
http://oyc.yale.edu/psychology/psyc-110/lecture-20

CHAPTER 14 – INCOME AND HAPPINESS

142.   • *Economic Growth and Subjective Well-Being: Re-Assessing the Easterlin Paradox*, Betsey Stevenson and Justin Wolfers, 2008. Brookings Panel on Economic Activity.
http://bpp.wharton.upenn.edu/betseys/papers/Happiness.pdf

        • *Income, Health, and Well-Being around the World: Evidence from the Gallup World Poll*, Angus Deaton, 2008. Journal of Economic Perspectives, 22(2). pp. 53-72.
http://www.aeaweb.org/articles.php?doi=10.1257/jep.22.2.53

143. *Does Inequality Make Us Unhappy?*, Jonah Lehrer, 2011. Wired.
http://www.wired.com/wiredscience/2011/11/does-inequality-make-us-unhappy/

144. *The Pursuit of Happiness: An Economy of Well-Being*, Carol Graham, 2011. Brookings Institution Press. p. 22.

145. *High income improves evaluation of life but not emotional well-being*, Daniel Kahneman and Angus Deaton, 2010. Proceedings of the National Academy of Sciences.
http://www.pnas.org/content/107/38/16489.full

CHAPTER 15 – HAPPINESS

146. Adapted from Spike Milligan's *Money can't buy you happiness but it does bring you a more pleasant form of misery* and many other variations.
http://thinkexist.com/quotation/money_can-t_buy_you_happiness_but_it_does_bring/220031.html

147. This quote is supposedly attributed to Jim Carrey, but I could only find one mildly reputable source. Regardless, I think it is a great quote.
http://goo.gl/7Am3s

148. *Genes, Economics, and Happiness*, Jan-Emmanuel De Neve, James H. Fowler, Bruno S. Frey, 2010. CESifo Working Paper Series 2946, CESifo Group Munich.
http://jhfowler.ucsd.edu/genes_economics_and_happiness.pdf

149. "Studies comparing identical twins with non-identical twins have helped to establish the heritability of many aspects of behaviour. Recent work suggests that about one third of the variation in people's happiness is heritable. Jan-Emmanuel De Neve has taken the study a step further, picking a popular suspect – the gene that encodes the serotonin-transporter protein, a molecule that shuffles a brain messenger called serotonin through cell membranes – and examined how variants of the 5-HTT gene affect levels of happiness. The serotonin-transporter gene comes in two functional variants – long and short – and people have two versions (known as alleles) of each gene, one from each parent. After examining genetic data from more than 2,500 participants in the National Longitudinal Study of Adolescent Health, De Neve found that people with one long allele were 8% more likely than those with none to describe themselves as very satisfied with life and those with two long alleles were 17% more likely of describing themselves as very satisfied. Interestingly enough, there is a notable variation across races with Asian Americans in the sample having on average 0.69 long genes, white Americans with 1.12, and black Americans with 1.47. 'It has long been suspected that this gene plays a role in mental health but this is the first study to show that it is instrumental in shaping our individual happiness levels,' writes De Neve. 'This finding helps to explain why we each have a unique baseline level of happiness and why some people tend to be naturally happier than others, and that is in no small part due to our individual genetic make-up.'", 2011. Slashdot.
    http://science.slashdot.org/story/11/10/18/0515236/the
    -genetics-of-happiness
150. Genetic engineering, personalised medicine, all fascinating fields to discuss, which will undoubtedly be at the centre of attention in a few years.
151. *Happiness is the Frequency, Not the Intensity, of Positive Versus Negative Affect*, Ed Diener, Ed Sandvik and William Pavot, 2009. Social Indicators Research Series, 2009, Volume 39. pp. 213-231.
    http://dx.doi.org/10.1007/978-90-481-2354-4_10
152. *Discoveries at the Diener's Lab*, Prof. Ed Diener, University of Illinois.
    http://internal.psychology.illinois.edu/
    ~ediener/discoveries.html
153. The example was adapted from the talk *Dan Gilbert asks: Why are we happy?*, Dan Gilbert, 2004. TED Global.
    http://www.ted.com/talks/dan_gilbert_asks_why_are_we_happy
    .html
154. *Dan Gilbert, Why are we happy?*, Dan Gilbert, 2004. TED Global.
    http://www.ted.com/talks/dan_gilbert_asks_why_are_we_happy
    .html. Emphasis mine.

CHAPTER 16 – WORK AND HAPPINESS

155. For a survey, see Darity and Goldsmith, 1996. Bj´orklund and Eriksson (1998) and Korpi (1997) provide evidence for Scandinavian countries, Blanchflower and Oswald (2004b) for the United Kingdom and the United States, Winkelmann and Winkelmann (1998) for Germany, and Ravallion and Lokshin (2001) for Russia.

156. *Unhappiness and Unemployment*, Andrew E. Clark and Andrew J. Oswald, 1994. The Economic Journal Vol. 104, No. 424 (May, 1994). pp. 648-659. http://www.jstor.org/stable/2234639

157. See, e.g., Winkelmann and Winkelmann 1998 for German panel data, or Marks and Fleming (1999) for Australian panel data, the latter considering in detail various effects on mental health.

158. For a survey, see Murphy and Athanasou (1999).

159. "There are some very interesting exceptions. For instance, we do not get used to noise. A lot of research suggests that if your environment is noisy, for example they are doing construction around you, you can not get used to it. Your happiness drops and it does not come back up. Your system cannot habituate to continued noise. We adapt to good things, winning the lottery, winning a prize, getting an 'A' in a course. We adapt, we get used to it, also with some surprising exceptions. One of the other surprises from happiness research is the effects of cosmetic surgery like breast enhancement and breast reduction. One of the big surprises is it makes people happier and they stay happier. And one explanation for this is how we look is very important. It is very important for how other people see us and how we see ourselves, and you never just get used to looking a certain way. So, if you look better it just makes you happier all the time." – *Psychology 110 Lecture 20 - The Good Life: Happiness*, prof. Paul Bloom. Yale University. http://oyc.yale.edu/psychology/psyc-110/lecture-20

160. Veum Goldsmith and Darity (1996).

161. Ruhm (2000).

162. Stutzer and Lalive (2004).

163. Clark and Oswald (1994).

164. *Handbook of Positive Psychology*, Jeanne Nakamura and Mihály Csíkszentmihályi, 2001. pp.89-101.

165. *Handbook of competence and motivation*, Mihály Csíkszentmihályi, Sami Abuhamdeh, and Jeanne Nakamura, 2005. Chapter 32 – Flow. http://academic.udayton.edu/jackbauer/CsikFlow.pdf

166. Bruno S. Frey (2008), Hamilton (2000), Ryan and Deci (2000).

167. Meier and Stutzer (2008).

168. *Table: The World's Happiest Countries*, 2010. Time Magazine.
    http://www.forbes.com/2010/07/14/world-happiest-countries
    -lifestyle-realestate-gallup-table.html?partner=popstories

169. *Average annual hours actually worked per worker.* OECD library, Organisation for Economic Co-operation and Development.
    http://stats.oecd.org/Index.aspx?DatasetCode=ANHRS

CHAPTER 17 – THE PURPOSE OF LIFE

170. *The Essential 20: Twenty Components of an Excellent Health Care Team*, Dianne Dukette and David Cornish, 2009. RoseDog Books. pp. 72-73.

171. *The New York Magazine Environmental Teach-In*, Elizabeth Barlow, 30 March 1970. New York Magazine. p. 30.
    http://books.google.com/books?id=cccDAAAAMBAJ
    &printsec=frontcover#PPA30,M1. Fuller was of course also an architect, an engineer, an author, a designer, a most notable systems theorist, and he is considered by many to be one of the greatest thinkers of the last century; having coined the terms "Spaceship Earth", ephemeralization, and synergetic, among others.

172. Philippe Beaudoin, 2012.
    https://plus.google.com/u/0/107988469357342173268/posts/
    2MVoo5KG1eP

173. *Rice University's 2012 commencement*, Salman Khan, 2012.
    http://www.khanacademy.org/talks-and-interviews/v/salman
    -khan-at-rice-university-s-2012-commencement

174. *80% Hate Their Jobs – But Should You Choose A Passion Or A Paycheck?*, 2010. Business Insider.
    http://articles.businessinsider.com/2010-10-04/strategy/
    30001895_1_new-job-passion-careers

CHAPTER 18 – PRACTICAL ADVICE FOR EVERYONE

175. Virtue. Wikipedia.
http://en.wikipedia.org/wiki/Virtue

176. Average Salary In United States.
http://www.averagesalarysurvey.com/article/average-salary
-in-united-states/15200316.aspx

177. *National Average Wage Index.* The United States Social Security Administration.
http://www.ssa.gov/oact/COLA/AWI.html

178. Regrettably, the origin of this quote is unknown, although it is generally cited as being Chinese. Over the years, the quote has been misattributed to Confucius, Lao Tzu, Laozi, and Guan Zhong. This is a Chinese Proverb, which loosely means "It is better to teach someone how to do something than to do it for them".
http://goo.gl/XdvT9

179. *Decline in fish stocks,* 1999. World Resources Institute.
http://www.wri.org/publication/content/8385

180. *iPhone 5 announcement: 3 important things to watch,* 2012. MSN Finance.
http://finance.ninemsn.com.au/newsbusiness/motley/
8531541/iphone-5-announcement-3-important-things-to-watch

181. *Why MIT decided to give away all its course materials via the Internet,* C. M. Vest, 2004. The Chronicle of Higher Education, 50(21), B20.

182. See *The Empathic Civilization: The Race to Global Consciousness in a World in Crisis,* Jeremy Rifkin, 2009. Tarcher.

183. Wolfram Alpha is an online service that answers factual queries directly by computing the answer from structured data, rather than providing a list of documents or web pages that might contain the answer as a search engine might. The goal is to "make all systematic knowledge immediately computable and accessible to everyone."
http://www.wolframalpha.com/about.html

184. *College 2.0: A Self-Appointed Teacher Runs a One-Man 'Academy' on YouTube,* Jeffrey R. Young, 2010. The Chronicle of Higher Education.
http://chronicle.com/article/A-Self-Appointed-Teacher
-Runs/65793/

185. Accelerating change. Wikipedia.
http://en.wikipedia.org/wiki/Accelerating_change

186. Journal of the American Dietetic Association.
http://eatright.org/cps/rde/xchg/ada/hs.xsl/home_7018_ENU
_HTML.htm

187. *FAO – Cattle ranching is encroaching on forests in Latin America*, 2005. Food and Agriculture Organization of the United Nations.
http://www.fao.org/newsroom/en/news/2005/102924/

188. *Ethics and Climate Change in Asia and the Pacific (ECCAP) Project*, Robert A. Kanaly, Lea Ivy O. Manzanero, Gerard Foley, Sivanandam Panneerselvam, Darryl Macer, 2010. Working Group 13 Report, Energy Flow, Environment and Ethical Implications for Meat Production.
http://unesdoc.unesco.org/images/0018/001897/189774e.pdf

189. *Livestock's Long Shadow: Environmental Issues and Options*, H. Steinfeld et al, 2006. Livestock, Environment and Development. Food and Agriculture Organization of the United Nations.
ftp://ftp.fao.org/docrep/fao/010/a0701e/a0701e00.pdf

190. *Water footprints of nations*, AK Chapagain, AY Hoekstra, 2004. Value of Water Research Report Series (UNESCO-IHE) 6.
http://www.waterfootprint.org/Reports/Report16Vol1.pdf

191. *Eating Lots of Red Meat Linked to Colon Cancer*. American Cancer Society.
http://209.135.47.118/docroot/NWS/content/NWS_1_1x_Eating
_Lots_of_Red_Meat_Linked_to_Colon_Cancer.asp

192. *Food, Nutrition, Physical Activity, and the Prevention of Cancer: a Global Perspective*, 2007. World Cancer Research Fund. p. 116.

193. *Breast Cancer Risk Linked To Red Meat, Study Finds*, Rob Stein, 2006. The Washington Post.
http://www.washingtonpost.com/wp-dyn/content/article/2006/
11/13/AR2006111300824.html

194. *Study Links Meat Consumption to Gastric Cancer*. National Cancer Institute.
http://www.cancer.gov/cancertopics/prevention-genetics
-causes/causes/meatconsumption

195. *Study links red meat to some cancers*. CNN.
http://www.cnn.com/US/9604/30/meat.cancer/

196. *Associations between diet and cancer, ischemic heart disease, and all-cause mortality in non-Hispanic white California Seventh-day Adventists*. The American journal of clinical nutrition 70 (3 Suppl): 532S-538S.
http://www.ajcn.org/cgi/pmidlookup?view=long&pmid=10479227

197. *Lung cancer risk and red meat consumption among Iowa women*, M. C. R. Alavanja et al, 2011. Lung Cancer 34.1. pp. 37-46.

198. *Relationship between meat intake and the development of acute coronary syndromes: the CARDIO2000 case-control study,* Kontogianni et al, 2007. European journal of clinical nutrition 62.2. pp. 171-177.

199. *Dietary Fat and Meat Intake in Relation to Risk of Type 2 Diabetes in Men,* R.M. Van Dam, W. C. Willett, E.B. Rimm, M. J. Stampfer, F. B. Hu, 2002. Diabetes Care 25 (3).

200. *Meat consumption is associated with obesity and central obesity among US adults,* Y. Wang, M. A. Beydoun, 2009. International Journal of Obesity 33 (6). pp. 621-628.

201. *Dietary risk factors for the development of inflammatory polyarthritis: evidence for a role of high level of red meat consumption,* D.J. Pattison et al, 2004. Arthritis & Rheumatism 50.12. pp. 3804-3812.

202. The Nest, an example of a Learning Thermostat.
http://www.nest.com

203. Hot Water Heater 'Blanket'.
http://www.greenandsave.com/utility_savings/gas/hot_water
_heater_blanket.html

204. Standby Power Reduction.
http://www.greenandsave.com/utility_savings/electric/standby
_power_reduction.html

205. Master ROI Table.
http://www.greenandsave.com/master_roi_table.html

206. *Integrative Design: A Disruptive Source of Expanding Returns to Investments in Energy Efficiency,* Amory Lovins, 2010. Rocky Mountain Institute.
http://www.rmi.org/Knowledge-Center/Library/2010-
09_IntegrativeDesign

207. *Solar and Nuclear Costs – The Historic Crossover,* John O. Blackburn and Sam Cunningham, 2010. Duke University. NC WARN: Waste Awareness & Reduction network.
http://www.ncwarn.org/wp-content/uploads/2010/07/NCW
-SolarReport_final1.pdf

208. *Mapping Solar Grid Parity,* John Farrell.
http://energyselfreliantstates.org/content/mapping-solar
-grid-parity

209. *Re-Mapping Solar Grid Parity,* John Farrell.
http://www.energyselfreliantstates.org/content/re-mapping
-solar-grid-parity-incentives

210. *Smaller, cheaper, faster: Does Moore's law apply to solar cells?*, Ramez Naam, 2011. Scientific American.
http://blogs.scientificamerican.com/guest-blog/2011/03/
16/smaller-cheaper-faster-does-moores-law-apply-to-solar
-cells/

211. *The True Cost Of Owning A Car*, 2008. Investopedia.
http://www.investopedia.com/articles/pf/08/cost-car
-ownership.asp#axzz1u18EBznk

212. *Road accident statistics in Europe*, 2007. CARE and national data, European Union.
http://ec.europa.eu/sverige/documents/traffic_press_stats
.pdf

213. *Cars and community – is it possible to have both?*, 2009.
http://makewealthhistory.org/2009/06/22/cars-and-community
-is-it-possible-to-have-both/

214. *National Obesity Trends*, 2010. CDC – National Center for Health Statistics.
http://www.cdc.gov/obesity/data/trends.html

215. *Over half the US will be obese by 2015*, YouTube.
http://www.youtube.com/watch?v=rXNe3LHlVxU

216. Peer-to-peer car rental. Wikipedia.
http://en.wikipedia.org/wiki/Peer-to-peer_car_rental

CHAPTER 19 – MAKING THE FUTURE

217. This quote is attributed to Peter Drucker, but many people expressed similar ideas – Alan Curtis Kay at a 1971 meeting of PARC said: "The best way to predict the future is to *invent* it". More recently, Peter Diamandis is famous for his phrase: "The best way to predict the future is to make it yourself."

218. Do not underestimate the importance of software. Most of the things that help us live better are software. Medical equipment, servers, personal computers, cellphones, electronics, street-lights, the Internet… think about how many things we take for granted, that could not exist without software.

219. Open Source. Wikipedia.
http://en.wikipedia.org/wiki/Open_source

220. *Can We Open Source Everything? The Future of the Open Philosophy.* University of Cambridge.
http://www.sms.cam.ac.uk/media/517352;jsessionid=62FE4CCB
3807753999235E2EA54E5009

221. LaTeX– a document preparation system.
     http://www.latex-project.org/
     Open at the source. Apple.
     http://www.apple.com/opensource/

222. *Kickstarter Expects To Provide More Funding To The Arts Than NEA*, Carl
     Franzen, 2012.
     http://idealab.talkingpointsmemo.com/2012/02/kickstarter
     -expects-to-provide-more-funding-to-the-arts-than-nea.php

223. *Marcin Jakubowski: Open-sourced blueprints for civilization*, Marcin Jak-
     ubowski. TED.
     http://www.ted.com/talks/marcin_jakubowski.html

224. Jimmy Wales interviewed by Miller, Rob 'Roblimo'. *Wikipedia Founder
     Jimmy Wales Responds*, 2004. Slashdot.
     http://slashdot.org/story/04/07/28/1351230/wikipedia
     -founder-jimmy-wales-responds

225. *Gin, Television, and Social Surplus*, Clay Shirky, 2010. Archived from the
     original on 2010-10-16.
     http://replay.web.archive.org/20101016111844/http://www
     .herecomeseverybody.org//2008//04//looking-for-the-mouse
     .html

226. *21 hours Why a shorter working week can help us all to flourish in the
     21st century*, Anna Coote, Jane Franklin and Andrew Simms, 2010. new
     economics foundation.
     http://neweconomics.org/sites/neweconomics.org/files/
     21_Hours.pdf

227. *Graham Hill: Why I'm a weekday vegetarian*, Graham Hill, 2010. TED.
     http://www.ted.com/talks/graham_hill_weekday_vegetarian
     .html

CHAPTER 20 – HOW TO BE HAPPY

228. Over the past few years, I noticed that new age spiritualists, mystics, various charlatans, self help gurus, and a whole range of pseudoscientists took the liberty of using the word quantum in very strange contexts, associating it with things that have nothing to with quantum mechanics, and bear no relationship with science in general. In case you are interested in what real quantum mechanics is, I suggest these excellent free online lectures by prof. Leonard Susskind from Stanford University.

- Course | Modern Physics: Quantum Mechanics
  http://www.youtube.com/playlist?list=PL84C10A9CB1D
  13841

- Course | Quantum Entanglements: Part 1 (Fall 2006)
  http://www.youtube.com/playlist?list=PLA27CEA1B8B27EB
  67

- Course | Quantum Entanglements: Part 3 (Spring 2007)
  http://www.youtube.com/playlist?list=PL5F9D6DB
  4231291BE

229. For the scientific evidence in support of the list, see *The Happiness Advantage: The Seven Principles of Positive Psychology That Fuel Success and Performance at Work*, Shawn Achor, 2010; and *Help!: How to Become Slightly Happier and Get a Bit More Done*, Oliver Burkeman, 2011.

230. *23 and ½ hours: What is the single best thing we can do for our health?*, Dr. Mike Evans.
http://www.youtube.com/watch?&v=aUaInS6HIGo

231. *If money doesn't make you happy, then you probably aren't spending it right*, Elizabeth W. Dunn, Daniel T. Gilbert, Timothy D. Wilson, 2011. Journal of Consumer Psychology.
http://www.wjh.harvard.edu/~dtg/DUNN%20GILBERT%20&%20WILSON
%20(2011).pdf

CHAPTER 21 – THE FUTURE IS BEAUTIFUL

232. Waking Life is an American animated film (rotoscoped based on live action), directed by Richard Linklater and released in 2001. The entire film was shot using digital video and then a team of artists using computers drew stylized lines and colors over each frame. The film focuses on the nature of dreams, consciousness, and existentialism. The title is a reference to philosopher

George Santayana's maxim: "Sanity is a madness put to good uses; waking life is a dream controlled". Wikipedia.
http://en.wikipedia.org/wiki/Waking_Life

APPENDIX A – HOW A FAMILY CAN LIVE BETTER BY SPENDING SMART

233. Consumer Reports says the average life expectancy of a new vehicle these days is around 8 years or 150,000 miles.
http://www.consumerreports.org

APPENDIX B – GROWTH

234. *Galactic-Scale Energy*, Prof. of Physics Tom Murphy, 2011. Do the Math.
http://physics.ucsd.edu/do-the-math/2011/07/galactic-scale-energy

235. Remember the rule of 70, the number of years to double a quantity at a fixed rate of growth, which was derived by taking 100 times the natural logarithms of 2. $100ln(2) = 69.3147181$. To get a factor of ten we use $100ln(10) = 230.258509$. Now take $230/100 = 2.3$. Therefore, 2.3% is the rate at which we get a factor of 10 increase every 100 years.

236. *Energy Use pro capita*, 2012. World Bank. Explore it interactively with Google Public Data.
http://goo.gl/olcMQ

237. *Galactic-Scale Energy*, Prof. of Physics Tom Murphy, 2011. Do the Math.

http://physics.ucsd.edu/do-the-math/2011/07/galactic-scale-energy/

238. *Can Economic Growth Last?*, Prof. Tom Murphy, 2011.
http://physics.ucsd.edu/do-the-math/2011/07/can-economic-growth-last

Bibliography

[1] Achor, Shawn. The Happiness Advantage: The Seven Principles of Positive Psychology That Fuel Success and Performance at Work (2010), Crown Business. ISBN-10: 0307591549, ISBN-13: 978-0307591548

[2] Brown, Lester R. Plan B 4.0: Mobilizing to Save Civilization (2009). W. W. Norton & Company. ISBN: 978-0393071030. http://www.earth-policy.org/books/pb4

[3] Brynjolfsson, Erik and McAfee, Andrew. Race Against the Machine: How the Digital Revolution is Accelerating Innovation, Driving Productivity, and Irreversibly Transforming Employment and the Economy (2012). Digital Frontier Press. ISBN-10: 0984725113, ISBN-13: 978-0984725113.

[4] Burkeman, Oliver. Help!: How to Become Slightly Happier and Get a Bit More Done (2011). Canongate Books Ltd. ISBN-10: 0857860267, ISBN-13: 978-0857860262.

[5] Cumberland, Richard. A Treatise of the Laws of Nature (2005). Indianapolis: Liberty Fund.

[6] Ford, Martin. The Lights in the Tunnel: Automation, Accelerating Technology and the Economy of the Future, (2009). ISBN-10: 1448659817, ISBN-13: 978-1448659814.

[7] Frey, Bruno S. Happiness: A Revolution in Economics, (2008). The MIT Press. ISBN-10: 0262062771, ISBN-13: 978-0262062770.

[8] Gilbert, Dan. Stumbling on Happiness (2007), Vintage. ISBN-10: 1400077427, ISBN-13: 978-1400077427.

[9] Graham, Carol. Happiness Around the World: The Paradox of Happy Peasants and Miserable Millionaires, (2010). Oxford University Press, USA. ISBN-10: 0199549052, ISBN-13: 978-0199549054.

[10] Graham, Carol. The Pursuit of Happiness: An Economy of Well-Being Publisher, (2011). Brookings Institution Press. ISBN-10: 0815721277, ISBN-13: 978-0815721277.

[11] Locke, John. Essay Concerning Human Understanding, Vol. 2 (1690). http://www.gutenberg.org/ebooks/10616

[12] Lucas, Stephen E., Justifying America: The Declaration of Independence as a Rhetorical Document. American Rhetoric: Context and Criticism, Thomas W. Benson, ed. Carbondale: Southern Illinois University Press. (1989).

[13] King, Martin Luther Jr. Remaining Awake Through a Great Revolution, sermon at the National Cathedral, 31 March 1968, published in A Testament of Hope: The Essential Writings and Speeches of Martin Luther King, Jr. (1990). HarperOne. ISBN-10: 0060646918, ISBN-13: 978-0060646912.

[14] Kurzweil, Ray. The Age of Spiritual Machines: When Computers Exceed Human Intelligence (1999). Viking Adult. ISBN 0-670-88217-8.

[15] Kurzweil, Ray. The Singularity Is Near: When Humans Transcend Biology (2005). Viking Adult. ISBN 978-0670033843.

[16] Pink, Daniel. Drive: The Surprising Truth About What Motivates Us (2009). Riverhead. ISBN-10: 1594488843, ISBN-13: 978-1594488849.

[17] Reich, Robert B. Aftershock: The Next Economy and America's Future (2011). ISBN-10: 0307476332, ISBN-13: 978-0307476333.

[18] Rifkin, Jeremy. The End of Work: The Decline of the Global Labor Force and the Dawn of the Post-Market Era (1995). Putnam Publishing Group. ISBN 0-87477-779-8.

[19] Rifkin, Jeremy. The Empathic Civilization: The Race to Global Consciousness In a World In Crisis (2010). Jeremy P. Tarcher. ISBN 1-58542-765-9.

[20] Rifkin, Jeremy. The Third Industrial Revolution: How Lateral Power Is Transforming Energy, the Economy, and the World (2011). Palgrave Macmillan. ISBN 978-0-230-11521-7.

[21] Sapolsky, Robert M. Why Zebras Don't Get Ulcers: An Updated Guide to Stress, Stress-Related Diseases, and Coping. (2006). The Norton Psychology Reader. Edited by Gary Marcus. New York: W. W. Norton & Company.

[22] Shirky, Clay. Here Comes Everybody: The Power of Organizing Without Organizations (2008). Penguin Group. ISBN 978-1594201530.

[23] Shirky, Clay. Cognitive Surplus: Creativity and Generosity in a Connected Age (2010). Penguin Group. ISBN 978-1594202537.

Made in the USA
San Bernardino, CA
28 August 2014